PATCHWORK
QUILTS *for the*
DOLLS' HOUSE

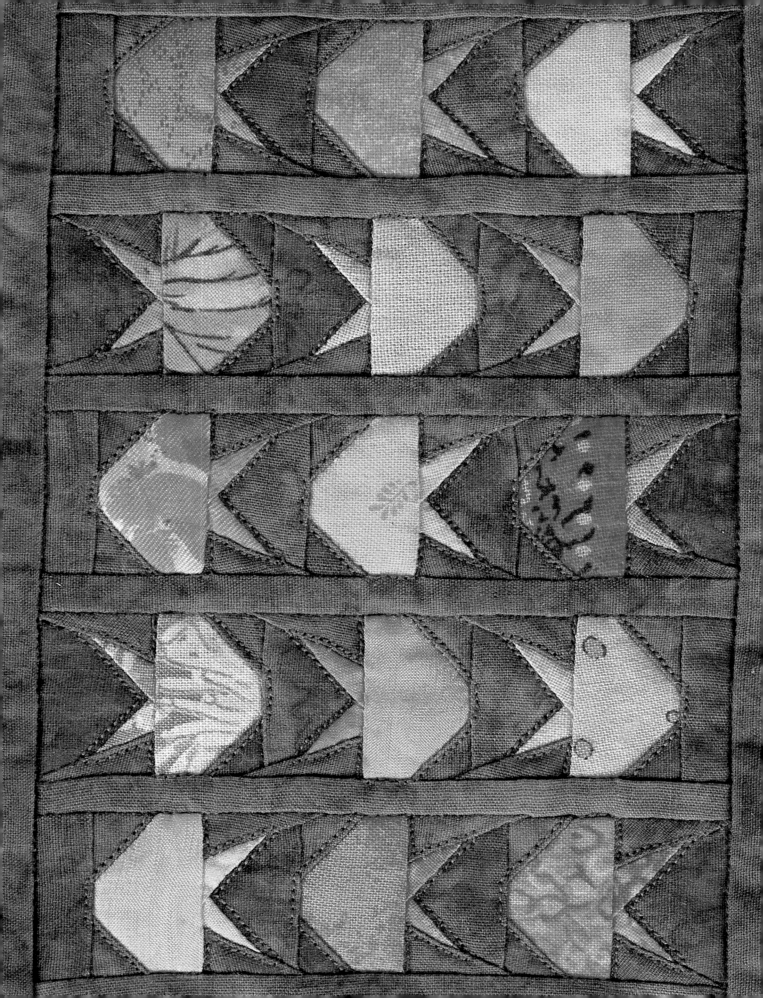

PATCHWORK QUILTS *for the* DOLLS' HOUSE

20 Projects in 1/12 scale

Sarah Williams

Guild of Master Craftsman Publications Ltd

First published 2002 by
Guild of Master Craftsman Publications Ltd
166 High Street, Lewes
East Sussex, BN7 1XN

Photographs by Christine Richardson
Illustrations by John Yates

ISBN 1 86108 305 X

British Cataloguing in Publication Data
A catalogue record of this book is available from the British Library.

Designed by John Hawkins
Typeface: Monotype Garamond

Colour origination by Viscan Graphics Pte Ltd (Singapore)
Printed and bound in Hong Kong by Printing Express Ltd

dedicated to

Susan and David, my parents
For loving me unconditionally, and teaching me to love 'for better, for worse'; for encouraging me to do what makes me happy, and always to do it well; and for showing me the satisfaction of creating something with my own hands.

acknowledgements

I would like to thank all the quilters who lent their beautiful quilts for the Gallery section; my friends in Precious Little Pieces for their encouragement as I experimented with miniature quilts; Gill Parris and Stephanie Horner at GMC Publications for all their help in writing the book; Josephine and Ruth, my sisters, for their unfailing love and support through good times and bad; Angela, Su, Leonie and Anita for their friendship and encouragement; and especially Rhys, for his love, advice and practical help. Thank you for encouraging me to follow my dreams.

The Publishers would like to thank Christiane Berridge for the loan of dolls' house furniture and Kangaroo, in Lewes, for the loan of materials used in the photographs.

a note about measurements

Measurements are in imperial, with approximate metric equivalents in brackets. Please note, however, that metric conversions may have been rounded up or down to the nearest equivalent. Only one set of measurements should be used, either imperial or metric, and the two must not be mixed.

contents

the QUILT PROJECTS

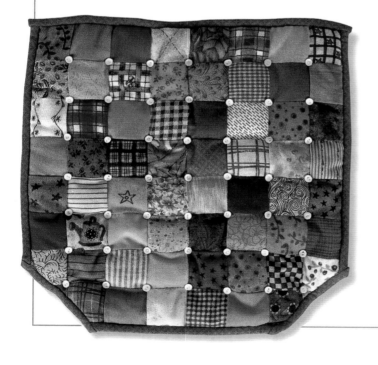

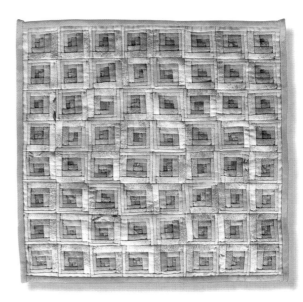

introduction

The miniature world of dolls' houses is a truly fascinating one, appealing to children and adults alike. For children, being able to act out scenes from their own lives and imaginations is rewarding play. For adults, the pleasure of decorating houses and creating miniature furniture can be very absorbing. The challenge of creating items which look real in 1/12 scale drives miniaturists to produce exquisite items which frequently astound others.

As a child, I spent countless hours playing with the dolls' house my father made for my sisters and me. When I wasn't playing with the dolls' house, I was sewing dolls' clothes. As I grew older, my interest in the dolls' house faded, and I spent more time on sewing and embroidery. In the early 1990s I started making patchwork quilts, inspired by the full-sized quilts my mother was making. The cot quilts I made for friends in those early years now seem huge compared with the tiny quilts in this book.

When my daughter Rebecca was born in 1994, I decided to give her a dolls' house for her third birthday, unaware that a whole world in miniature awaited me. I became fascinated by the adult hobby of miniatures, and spent many hours during 1997 renovating a dolls' house for my daughter. As my son Benjamin was born halfway through the year, I now look back in amazement that the house was ready in time.

The first miniature quilt I designed was for the main bedroom of Rebecca's dolls' house. Since then, I have made many more dolls' house quilts, which will eventually be displayed in a miniature quilt shop.

This book has grown from my love of sewing and fascination with miniatures. I hope you find inspiration within its pages, not just to reproduce the quilts that I have made, but perhaps also to try a quilt design of your own. Happy quilting!

There is hope in honest error; none in the ice perfections of the mere stylist.
Charles Rennie Mackintosh, 1902

GETTING STARTED

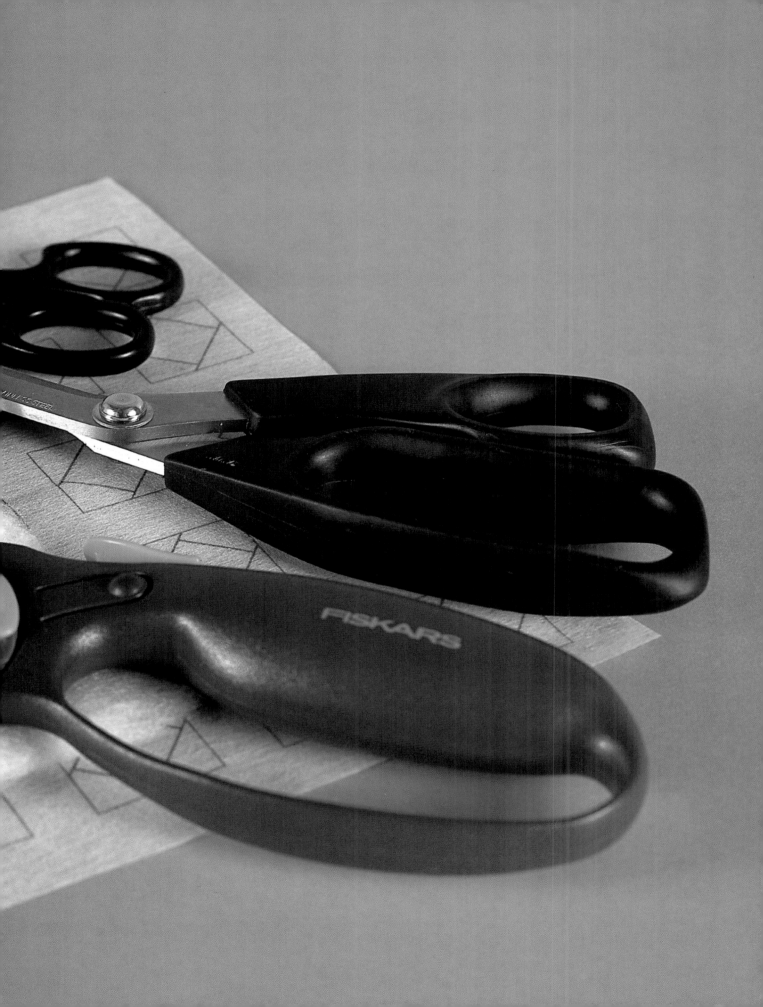

inspiration

Most of my quilts are inspired by full-size quilts that I've seen at exhibitions or in magazines, but inspiration for a quilt can come from many places. Perhaps you have seen a lovely fabric, and would like to use it in a quilt; or maybe you have decorated a bedroom in your dolls' house, so you want to make a quilt for that room. Wherever you get that first spark of an idea, try to note it down for future reference.

fabric

Fabric is the essence of the quilt and, as with many hobbies, my advice is to use the best materials you can afford. While you can make a miniature quilt from any fabrics, the best results will come from using natural fibres – cotton or silk – and from using lightweight fabrics.

One of the challenges of dolls' house quilting is making the quilt drape over a bed in the way a full-size quilt does. In the chapter Finishing Your Quilt (pages 39–58), you will find some suggestions on how to improve the way the quilt looks on a bed. Your choice of fabric, however, will make an enormous difference to the end result.

Some quilters use only cotton lawn or silk for their quilts. These produce a lovely soft quilt, but the range of colours and patterns available is very limited so, where possible, I use a lightweight fabric such as those for the main fabric of a quilt. For instance, the Blue Windmills quilt on page 123 has a silk background, while the Tropical Fish quilt on page 103 uses lightweight hand-dyed cotton. I also try to select a lightweight fabric for the backing. I can then use standard patchwork cottons to add colour and pattern, without the quilt becoming too stiff.

Why choose a cotton fabric for the patchwork pieces?
- **Cotton can be pressed flat and will stay flat after pressing**
- **Cotton is not slippery, so the patchwork pieces stay in place while you sew**
- **Cotton is less transparent than synthetic fabrics, therefore seam allowance shows less on the right side**
- **Cotton frays less than synthetic fabrics, which is important since seam allowances are very small in miniature quilts**

choosing fabrics

The largest piece of fabric you will use in a miniature quilt is 1in (2.5cm) square so, if you have been making full-sized quilts for some time, you may need to start looking at fabrics in a different way. Look for designs that lend themselves to small-scale work – small, overall prints of flowers are particularly suitable, or sometimes, geometric designs (but see overleaf). If you have a patchwork shop near your home, or can visit a quilt show, try to spend some time just feasting your eyes on the colours and patterns available.

Don't dismiss large-scale prints without looking at them carefully, however, as sometimes a large-scale print will have a few tiny motifs which you can cut out carefully. Often, too, the background colour is just right, and there may be plenty of background showing between the motifs.

Small-scale prints and florals

Large-scale prints

From top: solids, almost solids, hand dyes

Take care when selecting solid colours. I have found that the fabrics are often stiffer and harder to use than printed fabrics. You may be able to find hand-dyed fabrics which look almost solid, yet are a lighter weight. Alternatively, look for cotton lawn in solid colours, or use a printed fabric which looks almost solid.

5

Tone-on-tone prints

Many ranges of patchwork fabric include 'tone-on-tone' prints. This is where the design is the same colour as the background, but just a little darker or paler. Tone-on-tone prints look like a plain fabric from a distance, but add interest to the quilt when it is looked at closely. Since people will look at your dolls' house quilts very carefully, tone-on-tone fabrics are a good choice, provided the design (or part of the design) is small enough.

Geometric prints, such as spots and stripes, are hard to use in miniature patchwork, because the pieces of fabric need to be placed accurately, but I do sometimes use them, as they offer a pleasing contrast to floral prints (see the Country Squares quilt on page 69 for an example).

Geometric prints

HINT

Strange though it may seem, it is easier to make a great quilt using lots of different fabrics than just a few. If you use only six fabrics and one of them is not quite the right colour it will be very obvious but, among 20 or 30 fabrics, the one dubious choice will disappear. Look at the Red Log Cabin quilt on page 91 to see the effect of many different fabrics in one quilt.

washing fabric

Generally, we are advised to wash patchwork fabric before we use it. This is for a number of reasons: if you wash a quilt after it has been made, some of the colours may run; fabrics shrink a little when they are first washed, so washing the fabric before using it prevents puckering if the quilt is washed later; some fabrics are stiff because they contain a lot of size, and this disappears after washing, making the fabric softer. However, I must confess that I do not always wash fabric before I use it: it can be impractical if you work with small pieces and, if you are using quality fabrics, there should be little risk of the dye running.

So the choice of whether to wash fabrics before use or not is up to you, but I do recommend washing the following:

- Hand-dyed fabrics until the rinsing water runs clear

- Any fabric that may not be colour-fast, especially red fabrics, which are notorious for 'bleeding' into other fabrics

- Stiff fabrics, which need to drape well

- Cotton wadding (batting), as it softens after a hot hand wash

If you do decide to wash your fabric, it is best to hand wash each fabric separately in hand-hot water, so that you can see if the colour is running.

The problem of fabrics shrinking when washed is not a major issue with my finished quilts. Dolls' house quilts are not designed to be washed, and indeed the tiny seam allowances would not stand up well to washing.

fabric collecting

If you have been making patchwork quilts for a number of years, you will no doubt have a large 'stash' of fabrics already. All you need to do is select those most suitable for miniature quilts. But, if you are new to quilt-making, you may wonder where to start. How much fabric should you buy? How can you quickly increase the number of different fabrics in your collection?

You shouldn't have to travel too far to find suitable fabrics. Fabric or craft shops often stock patchwork equipment as well as fabrics. The owners are generally more than happy to help customers choose fabrics and may even suggest colour combinations that you would not have thought of.

One of the joys of dolls' house patchwork is that you do not need very much of any one fabric, so I usually buy the minimum cut off a roll that a shop will sell – often 8in (20cm), but occasionally 4in (10cm), which, of course, allows me to buy twice as many different fabrics for the same total outlay. If I plan to use a print as the main fabric in a quilt, or for backing, I will buy a 12in (30cm) piece.

I prefer to buy 'charm squares', when possible, rather than buying fabric off the roll. These are small pieces of many different fabrics cut up by the shop and sold in a pack. The pieces are usually around 5in (13cm) square – although the size varies from shop to shop – and the fabrics are often themed, say 1930s fabrics, purples, or brights. While the fabric works out more expensive per square inch than buying straight from the roll, the advantage is that you have an instant selection of fabrics for a quilt, and they may all look good together.

If you have the chance to attend a large quilt show, do go, as you will be able to stock up on fabrics, as well as gain many ideas on designing quilts and the use of colour. If you are new to quilting, don't be put off by the high standard of work – like most hobbies, the more you try, the better you become. The first quilts I made were cot quilts which I gave away to friends when they had babies. These were far simpler and less accurate than the miniature quilts in this book, yet I can see the complexity increasing and the choice of colours becoming bolder. I have kept photographs of them, and like to look back to see how I have progressed.

Mail-order fabric swatches

Buying fabric can become very expensive, so look for other ways to extend the range of fabrics you own. If you have friends who make quilts, perhaps you could swap fabrics with them. If they make full-sized quilts, ask for their scraps – they may be throwing away pieces of fabric that you could use.

Some mail-order fabric companies sell swatches of patchwork fabric, which are usually very small, often only 1½in (3.8cm) square. The Country Squares quilt on page 69 was made almost entirely from these tiny swatches.

A final source to consider is second-hand clothing. Not only is the fabric cheaper than new fabric from the shops, it has already been softened by wear. I used old silk tops for the backgrounds of both the Amish-style quilt on page 107 and the Kaleidoscope quilt on page 151.

interfacing

All of the quilts in this book, apart from the Appliqué Hearts quilt on page 95, have been made using the foundation piecing technique (see pages 25–38 for a detailed explanation of this technique). If you are familiar with foundation piecing, you will know that it involves drawing the block design on a foundation, usually paper for full-sized patchwork, and then sewing the fabric pieces onto the foundation, following the drawn lines. Once the block has been completed, the paper foundation is pulled out, leaving just the patchwork block.

I have found that it is not practical to use foundation papers in dolls' house quilts, since it would be almost impossible to remove all the paper from the completed block. Also, the seam allowance in dolls' house quilts is trimmed very close to the seam, often only $\frac{1}{8}$in (3mm) away, so the seams would not stand up to the tugging required to remove foundation papers.

For these reasons, I use lightweight sew-in interfacing as the foundation. It is very important that the interfacing is sew-in, not iron-on: if you use iron-on interfacing, the fabric pieces will stick to it when you press the seams, which you do not want to happen. You may need to experiment a little with different interfacings, until you find one that you are happy with: the very lightest interfacing may stretch a little as you sew, which would distort the shape of the block; however, if the interfacing is too heavy, it will make the quilt too stiff, and it will not drape well over the bed.

Interfacing, both plain and with foundation printed on it

wadding

To be a true quilt, there must be three layers – the patchwork top, the backing and, in between, a layer of wadding (batting). The wadding adds weight and warmth to the quilt, as well as giving a third dimension when the quilting stitches are added.

There are various different waddings available, both natural and synthetic. Some are easier to quilt through than others, and many are too stiff for our purposes. Each wadding has a different amount of 'loft', in other words, extent to which the wadding fibres spring up again after quilting.

For dolls' house quilts you need thin, soft wadding. For the quilts in this book, I have mostly used cotton wadding, silk wadding or pellon, which is a very thin polyester wadding. My favourite is silk wadding, because it is whisper-light and unbelievably soft. Unfortunately, it is very difficult to find, and rather more expensive than cotton or polyester wadding but, if you are able to, buy a small piece to try.

Many waddings are too thick for miniature quilts, so it is a good idea to peel the layers apart carefully and use just a thin layer. Even with silk wadding I separate layers and use only one-third of the thickness for a quilt.

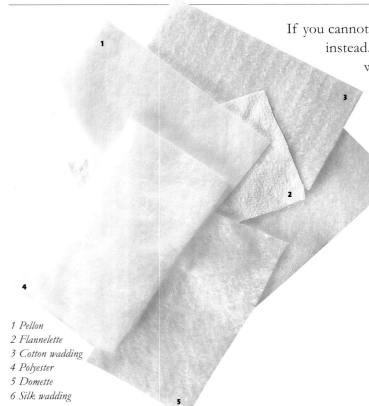

If you cannot find suitable wadding, try using a layer of flannelette instead. This drapes well, and gives the 'necessary' third layer, without adding stiffness.

I have indicated in each quilt project the sort of wadding I used, which will give you an idea of the different effects.

1 Pellon
2 Flannelette
3 Cotton wadding
4 Polyester
5 Domette
6 Silk wadding

A selection of sewing equipment

equipment

You will need basic sewing supplies for all of the quilts.

- Needles and pins
- Thimble (optional)
- Dressmaking scissors
- Embroidery scissors
- Rotary cutter and cutting board (optional)
- Thread
- Iron and ironing board
- Sewing machine (optional)

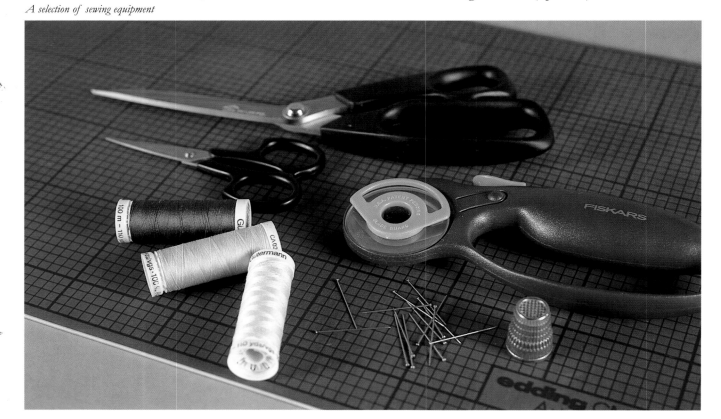

Needles and pins

If you are using a sewing machine, choose fine machine needles. I use a size 70/10 for most of my work, but choose a size 60/8 if the main fabric is silk or cotton lawn. That way, if I need to unpick a seam and re-sew it, the holes left by the needle disappear easily. Make sure that you change the needle in your machine regularly, as needles can become blunt, resulting in uneven seams. For hand sewing, I use a betweens needle in size 8 or 10. The finer the needle, the smaller the stitches you can make. Try using a gold-plated betweens needle in size 10 if you are striving for tiny quilting stitches.

The same rules apply to pins – use fine, sharp pins at all times, or they may leave holes in the fabric.

Thimble

The purpose of a thimble is to protect the finger which pushes the needle through the fabric (usually the middle finger of your right hand). If you do a lot of hand sewing you will know how useful it can be. Thimbles are available in metal, plastic, leather and ceramic. Choose whichever you find most comfortable and make sure it fits well.

I sometimes find a thimble awkward when I am trying to sew tiny stitches with small needles. If my finger becomes sore, I use a sticking plaster (bandaid) to protect the end and this is usually sufficient to keep me sewing for a while longer.

Scissors

You will need a pair of dressmaking scissors for cutting fabric, and embroidery scissors for snipping threads. Scissors should be kept very sharp. Although I have a rotary cutter and cutting board and find them invaluable for larger-scale work, I don't use them much for miniature patchwork. The exception is cutting strips for binding quilts, which is much easier with a rotary cutter than with scissors.

Thread

Choose good quality thread, in either cotton or cotton/polyester. Quilt books often recommend only using cotton thread, as polyester thread is stronger than cotton fabric and some old quilts have been damaged by polyester thread wearing away the fabric at the seams. This is especially the case where a quilt has been used often and washed frequently. However, this is rather less of a problem with dolls' house quilts, since the occupants of dolls' houses tend to rest peacefully in their beds! Unless you expect to have to wash the quilt regularly, using cotton/polyester thread should not be a problem.

A more difficult issue can be the colour of the thread. If the quilt will be all one colour, such as the Peach Ninepatch quilt on page 135, just choose a thread which blends well with the fabrics. If many colours will be used, a beige thread is a good choice for a pale quilt, while dark grey thread can be used for a dark quilt. Specific instructions on thread colour are given in some chapters.

Iron and ironing board

You will need a reliable steam iron for pressing fabric before use and for pressing all of the seams flat. The best irons for this purpose have a sharp point rather than a rounded end, as these fit better into small places. If you have a travel iron, this may also work well.

For miniature patchwork you rarely need to press large areas of fabric, except when pressing creases out of new or newly washed fabric. Most of the time I press on a sleeve board, set up on a table close to my sewing machine, rather than a full-size ironing board. I like to use a muslin cloth folded a few times to give a soft surface to press on, as this reduces the appearance of seam allowances on the right side of the quilt.

Sewing machine

I have made all of the quilt projects in this book using a sewing machine, because I particularly enjoy machine sewing. Most of the quilts can be made without a sewing machine, although the more complex quilts at the end of the book would take a long time to make if sewn by hand.

I find that seams sewn by machine are stronger and look more even than handsewn seams, and I can sew more quickly by machine than by hand. I use a special patchwork foot which is open at the front, allowing me to see exactly where the sewing machine needle will enter the fabric.

If you plan to make a number of dolls' house quilts, it is a real advantage to have a computerized sewing machine that you can set so that the needle finishes completely in or completely out of the work. This saves you having to crank the needle by hand every time you stop sewing. I also find the knee-lift feature on my sewing machine really useful, as it leaves me with both hands free to move the fabric.

If your sewing machine has a walking foot, it is worth spending time learning how to use it, as it makes machine quilting very straightforward.

quilting by hand

Many quilters do all their work by hand. If this is the method you choose, start and finish each seam with a backstitch rather than a knot, as knots are too bulky on miniature quilts. Using small running stitches, where the needle passes in and out of the work, sew each seam carefully.

When sewing by hand, handle the fabric gently, so that the seam allowance does not fray. Check often that you are sewing along the marked line, and try to keep your stitches an even size.

The big advantage of making miniature quilts by hand is that you can easily carry your work with you and do a little sewing when you have to wait somewhere.

A selection of beds

beds

There is an enormous variety of beds available from dolls' house shops and mail order suppliers – single beds, double beds, brass beds, wooden beds, simple beds, ornate beds – and many more. I really enjoyed choosing different beds to display the quilts in this book. I would advise, where possible, that you buy the bed before you make the quilt, as beds vary a surprising amount in their size.

The dimensions of the bed are not the only consideration when you are planning a quilt. Often, the bed has influenced the quilt design or colour that I have chosen. For instance, the ornately carved bed on page 134 seemed to need a traditional design, while the brass bed on page 150 called out for a subdued design in cream and gold. The lovely warm wood colour of the scroll bed on page 90 is accentuated by the red and cream quilt displayed on it.

If you already have a bed, consider what design and colours would suit it: a traditional design, such as Red Log Cabin or Peach Ninepatch (see pages 91 and 135), in muted colours, or a modern design like Riotous Pennants (page 111) in bright colours? You can, of course, take a traditional design and use bright colours, or select calmer colours yet use a modern design. It is your quilt and there are no rules, just guidelines and suggestions.

Style of bed

If you are buying a new bed before making a quilt, spend a few minutes thinking what style would be suitable. Obviously, if the bed is to go in a room in your dolls' house, you will be governed by the period of your house and will choose a bed that is appropriate. If, however, you plan the bed to be in a roombox, you have more choice.

The easiest style of bed for displaying quilts has both a headboard and a footboard. This is because the finished quilt drapes across the bed, so you can make a rectangular quilt, which is the easiest shape. In real life, beds with footboards often fail to show quilts to their best advantage, as the footboard stops you seeing the whole quilt. This is not a problem with dolls' houses, as you can look from above to see the quilt.

Many beds have a headboard at the top and posts at the foot. This requires a quilt with the bottom corners removed. You can choose to make a feature of the top and leave the sides and bottom plain, as I did for the Appliqué Hearts quilt on page 95, or you can make patchwork blocks for all parts of the quilt, like the Autumn Leaves quilt on page 155.

If the bed does not have a footboard, and does not have posts at the bottom, you can also make a rectangular quilt. You will, however, have some bulk at the bottom corners, which can be dealt with in the following ways:

- Cutting the bottom corners at an angle e.g. Country Squares quilt on page 69
- Folding the bottom part of the quilt underneath the mattress e.g. the Hearts quilt on page 117
- Leaving the quilt to drape over the end of the bed e.g. Sunset Log Cabin on page 131

Measuring the bed

A single bed will usually be around 3in (7.5cm) wide, while a double bed will be close to 4½in (11.2cm). Beds vary a lot in height; remember to include the mattress in the measurement. It is important to measure accurately, using a tape measure or ruler, especially if you are making a quilt to fit a bed with footposts.

Adjusting the pattern to fit the bed

Having measured the bed, you can decide what size you wish the quilt to be. You have some choice, because quilts do not need to reach all the way to the floor.

If you are making a rectangular quilt to fit a bed with headboard and footboard, the most important measurement is the length of the bed. If the bed measures just over 6in (15.2cm), as most do, you can use six 1in (2.5cm) blocks for the length. The quilt binding will add the extra ¼in (6mm) that you need. Alternatively, you could use five blocks, each just over 1in (2.5cm) square.

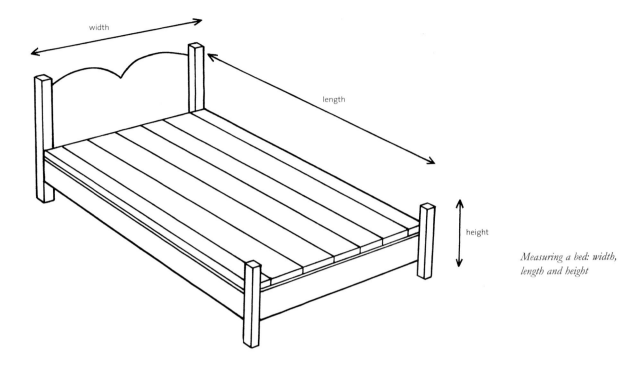

Measuring a bed: width, length and height

So, to calculate the size of each block, take the length of the bed, subtract ¼in (6mm) for the binding, and divide by the number of blocks you wish to make. For example, a bed 6¼in (16cm) long will need a quilt top measuring 6in (15.2cm).

6in (15.2cm) divided by six blocks makes 1in (2.5cm) blocks
OR 6in (15.2cm) divided by five blocks makes 1⅕in (3cm) blocks
OR 6in (15.2cm) divided by four blocks makes 1½in (3.8cm) blocks

Now that you have decided on the number of blocks to fill the length of the bed, consider the width. For any bed, the maximum width of the quilt will be the width of the bed plus twice the height, so that the quilt will drape to the floor on either side.

For a bed 4½in (11.5cm) wide and 2in (5cm) high, you would take the width plus twice the height to get 8½in wide (21.2cm). Again, you need to subtract ¼in (6mm) for the binding, giving you 8¼in (21cm). This is the maximum width, and anything from 7–8in (18–20cm) would be fine.

Depending on the size of block you have decided to make, you might need five, six, or seven blocks across the width. The table overleaf shows the measurements of a quilt, depending on the size of the block chosen. Notice how the number of blocks needed and the width of the quilt varies.

	Number of blocks			Measurements	
	Down	Across	Total	Length	Width
1in (2.5cm) blocks	6	7	42	6¼in (16cm)	7¼in (18.5cm)
1⅕in (3cm) blocks	5	6	30	6¼in (16cm)	7½in (19cm)
1½in (3.8cm) blocks	4	5	20	6¼in (16cm)	7¾in (19.5cm)

The size of block you decide to make will depend partly on the size you want your finished quilt to be, and partly on how many blocks you wish to make. When you are first starting miniature patchwork, it is helpful to make larger blocks as these are less fiddly than 1in (2.5cm) blocks. Any of the patterns can be altered in size by enlarging them on a photocopier. As you become more confident, you can move to 1in (2.5cm) blocks, or even smaller on occasion.

Beds with footposts
Adjusting patterns for beds with footposts is more awkward, because the width of the bed is important as well as the length. It is easiest to think of the quilt as a rectangle (length times width) and then add borders on to the sides and the bottom.

Quilt top with sides and bottom

For instance, if your bed is 6¼in long by 4½in wide (16cm by 11.5cm) you could use 1in (2.5cm) blocks arranged in six rows of four blocks for the quilt top. The binding will add the extra ¼in (6mm) to the length and the extra ½in (12mm) to the width. You will then need to make blocks for the side and bottom borders.

Single beds which are only 3in (7.5cm) wide can be difficult, since you need to allow ¼–½in (6–12mm) for the binding on the bottom border. Subtracting this from 3in (7.5cm) leaves at most 2¾in (7cm) for the patchwork blocks. You could choose to make the quilt top only two blocks wide, with each block almost 1½in (3.8cm) square. Or, as I have done in the Autumn Leaves quilt on page 155 and the Stars quilt on page 145, you could use ⅞in (2.3cm) blocks. This gives three blocks across the quilt top and seven blocks down. Again, add borders to the sides and bottom – the quilt projects give more details on how to do this.

The table below shows the effect of choosing either two or three blocks across the width of the quilt top. While two blocks across is much less work (only eight blocks to make instead of 21) the quilt will be a little short on the bed, so will need a wide binding at the top.

	Number of blocks			Measurements	
	Down	Across	Total	Length	Width
⅞ in (2.3cm) blocks	7	3	21	6⅛in (15.5cm)	2⅝in (6.7cm)
1⅜in (3.5cm) blocks	4	2	8	5½in (14cm)	2¾in (7cm)

If your bed has footposts, the other possibility would be to choose a design with sashing strips in between the blocks, such as the Tropical Fish quilt on page 103. You could make each block ⅞in square (2.2cm) and then alter the width of the sashing strips until your quilt top is the correct width.

COLOUR

Often the first thing I notice about a quilt is its colour: some quilts are bright and impossible to ignore, while others use more muted colours. Some colour combinations are restful, while others are so vibrant that our hearts race when we see them. Then, of course, there are colours that evoke specific memories or associations – red, white and blue is a patriotic colour scheme for many people, while shades of green remind us of gardens.

In this chapter I aim to give an introduction to colour theory. If you already know how to choose colours for a quilt, feel free to skip to the next chapter. However, if you have sometimes felt that your quilts lacked impact, or if you are new to quiltmaking, please spend a little time considering how colour choices affect the mood of a quilt.

The Bibliography on page 178 lists a few books on colour theory which I found helpful and you could check your local library to see if they stock copies of any of these.

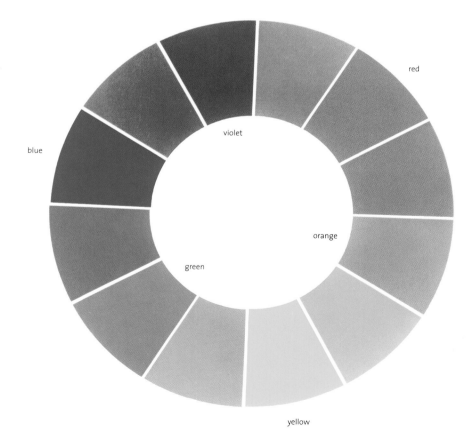

A colour wheel

red

violet

blue

orange

green

yellow

colour wheel

When considering colour, it can be helpful to look at a colour wheel. The primary colours of red, yellow and blue are evenly spaced around the circle, with secondary colours of orange, green and violet in between. Further blending of the colours is possible, giving 12 distinct colours on the basic colour wheel.

The colours shown are pure colours, that is, they haven't been diluted with white or darkened with black. Nor have they been softened by adding grey.

Fabric colour wheel

To learn a little more about colour theory, you might like to try making your own fabric colour wheel, like the one pictured below. To do this, select 12 fabrics which match the 12 colours on the wheel. You can choose to use solid fabrics, if you have a good selection, or patterned fabrics which are predominantly the required colour. The process of selecting fabrics and comparing them with each other is very valuable and you will see how colours change as they are put next to others in the wheel.

Try selecting the three primary colours first – red, blue and yellow – and look for the reddest red, the bluest blue and the yellowest yellow. Then add in the secondary colours of orange, green and violet. As you add the tertiary colours, you may find that you need to change one of the primary or secondary colours. For instance, as I worked on my fabric choices, I found that my first choice for yellow was too green when I saw it next to yellow-green.

A fabric colour wheel

As you look at a colour wheel, each colour should be an equal mix of the two colours on either side. Thus blue-green should be an equal mix of blue and green. This can be hard to achieve when you are selecting fabrics from your stash but, even if your final colour wheel is slightly imperfect, the process of making it is valuable.

Warm and cool colours

You can split the colours on the colour wheel into two groups – warm colours and cool colours. Warm colours are reds, yellows and oranges, and they remind us of the sun or a blazing log fire. Cool colours, on the other hand, are the colours of sea, sky and grass – all shades of blue and green. Warm colours are exciting and passionate, while cool colours are more relaxed and calming.

Neutral fabric samples

When you choose fabrics for your quilts, consider the effect you wish to produce. Often quilts are made from cool colours, as these fit the relaxing ambience of a bedroom. But if the quilt is to be the focal point of the room, you might prefer a more lively colour scheme.

Neutrals

Neutral fabrics technically contain none of the colours found on the colour wheel – they are 'non-colours'. So black, white and grey are all neutrals. Their role is to provide a rest from the colour and to draw attention to the coloured fabrics in a quilt. Quilters also treat beige as neutral, and use it widely as a background colour.

Colour value

As already mentioned, the colours found on a colour wheel are pure colours. Adding white, black or grey changes the colour and the effect it has in a quilt. This is referred to as changing the value of the colour. When you add white to a colour it becomes paler, and more restful. Most of the fabrics in Sunset Log Cabin on page 131 are pure colours with white added.

Adding black to a colour darkens it and makes it stronger. Adding grey softens a pure colour and reduces its intensity. The Peach Ninepatch quilt on page 135 is a good example of a pure colour – red – made paler by adding white and also duller by adding grey.

choosing colours for a quilt

Wherever the inspiration for your quilt comes from, it is likely that you have one or two colours in mind, so you then need to consider which other colours to add. Referring to the colour wheel can help but here I explain a few colour combinations which always work well.

Monochromatic

In a monochromatic colour scheme, there is only one colour used, or one colour plus neutrals. The Red Log Cabin quilt on page 91 is a monochromatic colour scheme, as the only colours used are red and cream. However, this is still an interesting quilt, because there are so many different reds and creams used, so monochromatic needn't mean boring.

Analogous

A quilt made with three adjacent colours on the colour wheel will always look good. For instance, blue, blue-green and green together will give a pleasing effect. So an easy way to choose colours is to take your main colour, and add in the colour found on either side of it on the colour wheel.

Fabric samples showing pure purple; purple with black added (dark purple); purple with white added (pale purple); purple with grey added (dull purple)

21

Blue, blue-green and green fabric samples

Complementary

Sometimes you may find that your quilts lack impact. If they are pleasant to look at but not very exciting, you may need to add an accent colour. In our example of using three adjacent colours on the colour wheel, the accent colour to choose is directly opposite these three on the wheel. For instance, if you are using blue, blue-green and green, choose red-orange as your accent. You will only need a very little of the accent colour to add excitement to your quilt (see fabric samples on facing page).

Many dramatic quilts are made with colours from opposite sides of the colour wheel. For instance, the Riotous Pennants quilt on page 111 is particularly vibrant because it uses equal quantities of warm and cool colours. The oranges and yellows seem almost to fight with the greens and blues.

Dominant colours

As you start to experiment with colours, you will see that some colours seem to stand out more than others. These are called dominant colours. It can be helpful to know that warm colours, dark colours and pure colours are dominant and will advance from the surface of the quilt. As you might imagine, cool colours, pale colours and colours toned down with grey will all recede.

Try looking at the quilts in this book, and see which colours stand out. Notice the background colour of the quilt, and try to decide why a particular colour is dominant. Yellow is the strongest colour in your quilt stash, so it needs to be used carefully. I like using yellow in quilts, but be aware that the finished quilt will not be restful if it has a lot of yellow in it.

Brown

You will notice that brown does not appear on the colour wheel. That is because brown is a combination of all three primary colours. Imagine mixing paints with a young child. You combine red and yellow to make orange, blue and yellow to make green and finally red and blue to make purple. Then your child decides to mix them all together, and you get ... brown.

Brown doesn't count as a neutral colour, because it is too strong. However, it is a restful colour, perhaps because we associate it with the earth. Quilters have chosen brown as a main colour for their quilts for many decades, partly because early fabric dying produced many brown shades. Look at the Noah's Ark quilt on page 73 to see the effect of a predominantly brown quilt.

Background colours

The colour you choose for the background of a quilt also affects the mood of the finished quilt. Bearing in mind that pale and cool colours recede, a cream background will always make the motifs stand out. Cream and white also soften colours, while dark backgrounds can make colours more vivid. The quilt on page 95 has red and pink hearts appliquéd onto a cream silk background, which produces a soft and feminine quilt. Compare this with the Stars quilt on page 145, where the black background makes the bright stars leap forward into view.

Blue, blue-green, green and red-orange fabric samples

It is really worth spending some time experimenting with different background colours. For instance, when I was making the Autumn Leaves quilt on page 155, I was sure that I wanted a brown background, so that it would seem as though the leaves had fallen onto bare earth. Although the concept was great, when I started making some leaf blocks with a brown background I realised that the leaves weren't standing out enough. Changing to a much paler background emphasized the leaf motif and showed the autumn colours much better.

Colour contrast

Whether you choose a monochromatic, analogous or complementary colour scheme, you need to ensure some contrast between the fabrics. This could be a value contrast, using paler and darker shades of the same colour. Or contrasting intensity, where some fabrics are pure colours and others are grey tones of the same colour. Try to ensure some contrast of print by using tone-on-tone fabrics, hand-dyes and small-scale prints in the same quilt. Perhaps you could add a geometric print as a contrast to floral prints.

Look at paintings and full-scale quilts for inspiration. Analyse the colours used, and try to work out what you like about the combination. Try experimenting with different colours before you make a quilt, either by just placing the fabrics next to each other or by making up sample blocks in different colourways. Add a small piece of a contrasting fabric to see if you like the effect – you can always take it away again. And remember that colour preference is personal; what you love, someone else may really dislike, so don't be put off by other people's comments as you try different colours in your quiltmaking.

FOUNDATION PIECING

Patchwork originated as a thrifty way of using up scraps of fabric, or of recycling worn clothing. Early patchwork was done over paper templates, which were removed when the patches had been sewn together by hand. This type of patchwork is still popular today, and is generally known as English patchwork. There are some exquisite miniature quilts made by this method, including six different hexagon quilts shown in the Gallery section (see pages 164, 165, 166, 171, 173 and 175).

With the advent of the sewing machine, other types of patchwork became possible. Early American settlers developed many designs using strips, squares and triangles, which were cut out accurately and sewn together by machine. This has become known as American patchwork. Examples of traditional designs are Peach Ninepatch on page 135, Flying Geese on page 127 and Red Log Cabin on page 91.

For the dolls' house enthusiast, both English and American patchwork have one big disadvantage – they require fabric to be cut accurately before it is sewn. While it is not difficult to cut out a 3in (7.5cm) hexagon, cutting the same shape only ¼in (6mm) across is a real challenge. Similarly, cutting squares, triangles or strips in full scale is not hard, especially with tools like rotary cutters and quilting rulers to help but, in 1/12 scale, cutting out small pieces then sewing them together with accurate seam allowances is very difficult.

The solution to this problem is to use foundation piecing, where the design is drawn on a 'foundation' of paper or fabric, and the pieces are joined together by sewing along the lines by hand or machine. Many traditional designs can be sewn using this method, and many new designs have been developed.

The main advantage of foundation piecing is that the fabric does not have to be cut accurately. Instead, you take fabric a little larger than the finished size, sew it in place, then trim it to size.

If you are familiar with foundation piecing, just skim through this chapter, making a note of anything that seems different from your normal practice. There is a summary of the important points at the end of the chapter. If you are new to foundation piecing, I recommend working through the two examples given here before you start on a miniature quilt.

example one – log cabin

The log cabin design used in this example is a 2in (5cm) block, which is larger than you would normally use in a dolls' house. However, if this is your first attempt at miniature patchwork using foundation piecing, it is sensible to start with an easy example and then progress to more detailed work.

I have used lots of different colours of fabric in this example, to make it easier for you to see which fabric has been added at each step. I have also sewn the seams with contrasting thread so that they are visible, but you may prefer to choose colours that blend more harmoniously. The general rule in log cabin is that half of the block uses dark fabric while the other half uses light. The central square is often red, to represent fire warming the house.

Log cabin template (actual size)

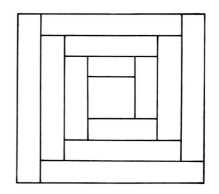

Log cabin fabric-piecing sequence

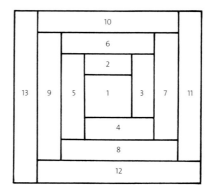

1 Start by tracing the log cabin design onto fine interfacing or fine white cotton fabric. Use a sharp pencil or a fabric marker and a ruler to help keep your lines straight. If you wish, you can write the numbers which indicate the order of adding fabric pieces to the foundations. Alternatively, just refer to the diagram in the book as you sew. Whether or not you write on the numbers, I recommend writing 'top' above the drawn lines to indicate the top of the block. This will also help you to distinguish the right and wrong sides of the foundation.

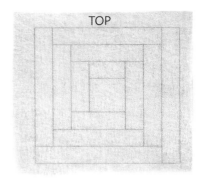

Interfacing marked with log cabin design

2 Cut out a square of fabric for the centre of the block. This needs to be a little larger than the finished square, so cut it approximately 1in (2.5cm) square. Place the wrong side of the fabric against the wrong side of the foundation. You may need to hold the foundation and fabric up to the light to check that the fabric is covering the central square.

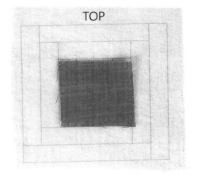

Red fabric in centre

3 Now cut a few strips of fabric, a mix of dark and light prints, each ⅝in (1.6cm) wide. Choose one of the light fabrics to be piece number 2 and place this on top of the central square, right sides together. Use a pin to hold the two pieces onto the foundation.

Red fabric plus green pinned in place

4 Turn the foundation over so that the lines you have drawn are visible. Sew along the line which joins pieces 1 and 2, removing the pin as you sew. Start and finish the seam two or three stitches beyond the line so that the seam will not come undone. Use a shorter stitch length than normal, ideally around 16 stitches to 1in (2.5cm). If you have a sewing machine which uses metric stitch length, this means each stitch will be 1.5mm long.

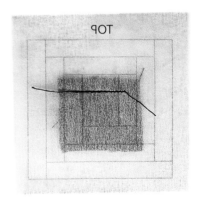

The reverse side, with black stitching showing

Trimmed fabric, with interfacing folded back

5 Next, trim the seam allowance of the seam you have just sewn. To do this, fold the foundation fabric safely out of the way, then trim the seam to ⅛in (3mm).

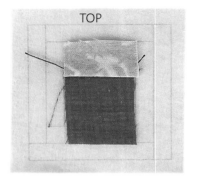

Red and green fabrics, pressed flat

6 On the right side, press piece 2 into its correct position with your fingers. Hold the block up to the light to check that the piece extends at least ⅛in (3mm) all round the printed lines. If necessary, undo the seam and reposition piece 2, then re-sew. When you are happy with its placement, press firmly with a dry iron.

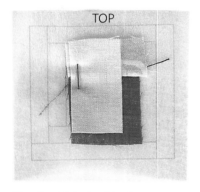

The yellow fabric pinned in place

7 Next, attach piece 3 (also a light-coloured fabric) in the same way as piece 2 but, this time, add the new fabric at the side rather than the top of the block.

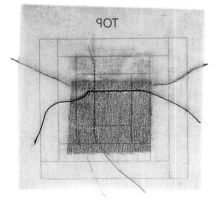

The reverse side, showing the turquoise thread

8 I have used turquoise thread to sew on piece 3. You can see that the seam I have sewn is two stitches longer than the printed line at the beginning and end of the seam.

9 Again, trim the seam carefully, folding the foundation fabric to prevent your scissors from snipping it accidentally.

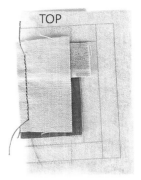

The yellow fabric, trimmed

10 Press piece 3 into its correct position.

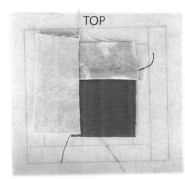

The red, green and yellow fabric, pressed flat

11 Add dark fabric strips to the bottom and right side of the block. Each time you add new fabric, trim the seam allowances carefully, otherwise there will be too much bulk at the seams. If you have made your seams too long, that is, more than three stitches longer than the printed line, you will have to unpick a little of the seam before you can trim the seam allowances of the next piece.

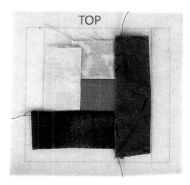

The red, green, yellow, blue and purple fabric pressed flat

12 Keep adding the log cabin strips, remembering to make half of the block light and half dark. As this is a sample block, the colour choice does not matter. Concentrate on sewing accurately along the lines you have drawn.

The block, nearly finished

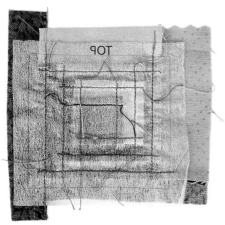

The back of finished block, showing loose threads

13 When all the pieces are in place, the back of the work may look a little messy.

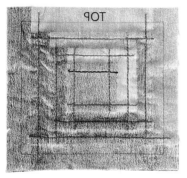

The back of the finished block, with the ends of thread trimmed

14 Trim the loose ends of thread and neaten the edges of the block.

The front of the finished block

15 Press the block carefully. If you have chosen more harmonious fabrics than my sample, you may decide to frame the block as a miniature picture. Alternatively, you could make a number of other blocks and turn them into a doll's or teddy bear's quilt.

example two – fish block

This design is a little more awkward than the first example, as it includes triangles, but the general approach is the same.

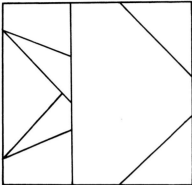

Fish template (actual size)

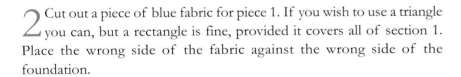

Fabric-piecing sequence

1 Trace the design onto fine interfacing or fine white cotton fabric, using a sharp pencil or a fabric marker.

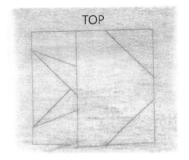

Interfacing marked with fish design

2 Cut out a piece of blue fabric for piece 1. If you wish to use a triangle you can, but a rectangle is fine, provided it covers all of section 1. Place the wrong side of the fabric against the wrong side of the foundation.

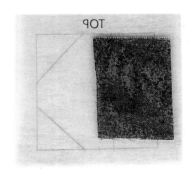

Blue fabric on the printed block

3 Now cut a 1¼in (3cm) square of brightly coloured fabric for the tail, then cut it across the diagonal to make two triangles. Place one triangle on top of the blue fabric, right sides together, and use a pin to hold the two pieces on the foundation. The seam you will be sewing joins piece 2 to piece 1. Most of the tail fabric needs to be on top of piece 1 at this stage so that, after you have sewn the seam, the fabric can be flipped over to cover the tail section of the design.

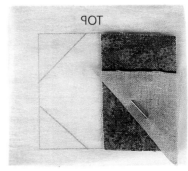

Blue fabric with orange fabric pinned in place

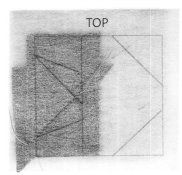

Seam sewn with green thread

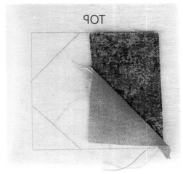

Blue and orange fabric pressed flat

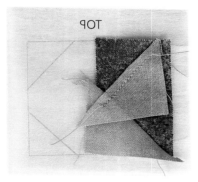

Blue and orange fabric pressed flat, second orange piece sewn in place

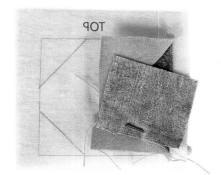

Square of blue fabric pinned in place

4 Turn the foundation over, so that the lines you have drawn are visible. Sew along the line connecting pieces 1 and 2, removing the pin as you sew. Remember to start and finish the seam two or three stitches beyond the line.

5 Now trim the seam allowance, being careful to fold the foundation fabric out of the way. Check that piece 2 is in the correct position then press firmly with a dry iron.

6 Sew the second tail piece in the same way.

7 Pieces 4 and 5 are a little awkward, so it is best to start with large rectangles then trim to size after sewing. Cut two rectangles from the blue fabric, each 1¼ × 1in (3 × 2.5cm). Position a long side of the rectangle next to the tail piece and sew in place.

8 Hold the block up to a light source to check that the fabric extends at least ⅛in (3mm) beyond the edges of the design. If you need to move a piece of fabric, unpick the seam carefully, adjust the position of the fabric, then re-sew.

The fish tail completed

9 Piece 6 is the main body of the fish. Take a rectangle of bright fabric 2¼ × 1½in (5.6 × 3.8cm) and pin it on top of the tail, right side down.

Orange fabric pinned in place

10 Sew the long seam, then trim and press.

The completed tail plus orange fabric pressed flat

11 The final two pieces require a 1¼in (3cm) square of blue fabric, cut into two triangles. Sew these in place, so that they cover the corner triangles.

Blue triangles sewn in place

The completed fish block

Fish block with border strips and eye

12 Press the final pieces into their correct positions.

13 Trim the loose ends of thread and press the block carefully. You can, if you wish, add border strips in the blue fabric and draw an eye with a fabric marker or embroider a French knot.

Fish greetings card

You could turn this sample block into a greetings card or pin cushion. A few dots of pearly fabric paint make convincing bubbles.

If you found the fish design difficult to stitch, I suggest you start with one of the easier quilt designs in this book which only uses squares and rectangles. When you have made one or two simple quilts, it would be a good idea to try sewing the fish block again.

sewing blocks for a whole quilt

Now that you know the basics of foundation piecing, there are a few tips I can offer to make sewing multiple blocks a little easier.

♦ Make sure that your sewing area is comfortable and that you have all your equipment ready to hand. If you have a room devoted to your hobby, this is ideal. My working area, however, is just a small desk in the corner of the dining room. My family knows not to touch anything on my desk, and I can use the dining room table when I need to spread out a little.

♦ I use small plastic bags to store my foundations, small pieces of fabric I have cut in preparation for sewing and my completed blocks. This way my sewing area remains organized, and there is less chance of losing anything.

Plastic bags with fabric etc inside

♦ I choose to sew a few blocks at a time, in batches of perhaps seven or eight. This reduces the amount of moving from the sewing machine to the ironing board, so it speeds up the process. I also find that if I am sewing a complex block, where I have to think before positioning each piece of fabric, sewing a few blocks at a time becomes more efficient.

♦ It is best to sew for only one hour at a time, as miniature patchwork requires a lot of concentration. Make sure you take regular breaks from your sewing, and consider doing a few stretching exercises to loosen stiff muscles. It is also important to focus on a distant object as your eyes have been focusing at a close distance for a while.

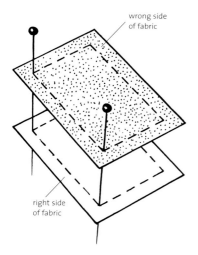

wrong side
of fabric

right side
of fabric

Pinning segments together

blocks made of two segments

Some of the more complex patterns in this book require blocks to be made in two segments which are then joined together, for example Autumn Leaves on page 155. Make up the two parts of the block using the general instructions already described, then pin them together carefully, placing pins vertically through both segments at the corners. You will need to adjust the position of the segments until you have a good match.

Pin, then sew, the joining seam slowly and carefully, then press the seams open. In a complex block, I often sew this central seam by hand, even though the rest of the quilt may be sewn by machine.

drawing foundations by hand

If you have access to a computer, please read Using a Computer on pages 59–65, as this explains how your computer can be used to produce foundations. Here, I explain how to draw the foundations for a complete quilt by hand.

The foundations for full-size patchwork are often drawn on paper, which is removed after the fabric has been sewn in place. For miniature patchwork I recommend using fine, woven interfacing as the foundation rather than paper. This is because it is difficult to remove paper from miniature blocks without damaging them, as the seam allowances are so small.

It is important that the interfacing is not stiff, and also that it does not stretch as you sew. The interfacing must be sew-in, not iron-on – check with a shop assistant if you are unsure. If you use iron-on interfacing, the fabric pieces will stick to it when you press the seams. Try to find a fabric shop with a range of interfacings. You may wish to buy a small amount of a few different interfacings and see how they cope with drawn foundations.

With fine interfacing it is possible to trace the foundation pattern directly from this book, although you may prefer to make a photocopy of the pattern first, to prevent damage to the pages.

There are various ways of marking your foundations. Whichever method you choose, you are aiming for all the blocks to be identical. If you have errors in your foundations, the finished quilt will look uneven.

- Mark each block directly on the interfacing using a sharp pencil or fine permanent marker to draw the lines. Mechanical pencils work well but you have to work carefully to avoid ripping the interfacing.

- Make a stack of four pieces of interfacing separated by dressmakers' carbon paper. Top the stack with a sheet of paper, and draw the pattern onto this. You can use a

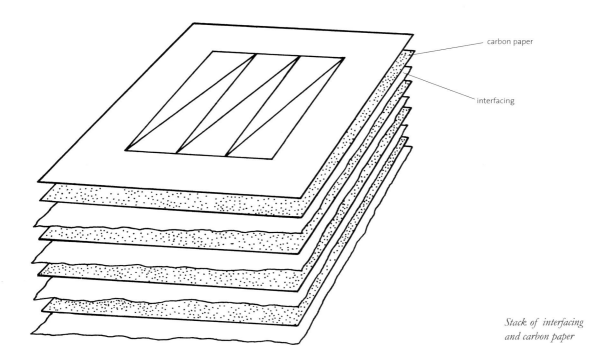

carbon paper

interfacing

Stack of interfacing and carbon paper

photocopy of the design, and trace over all of the lines. You will need to press very hard to ensure that the image appears on all layers of interfacing.

- Draw the pattern on baking parchment using a hot-iron transfer pen. The design can then be transferred onto the interfacing by ironing carefully. You will need to redraw the pattern several times, as each image will only transfer a few times.

making cardboard templates

Although I have used the foundation-piecing technique for most of the quilts, for simple square blocks such as the Country Squares quilt on page 69 it is often easier to draw round a template. Check the measurements of the block you are making, then draw a square of the correct size onto cardboard. You can check if your square is accurate by measuring the diagonals – a true square has diagonals the same size as each other.

Cut out the square, then draw round it onto paper. Check the measurements of the square you have drawn, as you may find it is now slightly too big. If this is the case, trim your cardboard template a tiny amount until it is the right size. Draw round the template onto the back of the fabrics you have chosen for your quilt. If you are using a striped or checked fabric, make sure one edge of the square template is lined up accurately with the pattern.

quick piecing techniques, using a sewing machine

Many of the quick patchwork techniques developed for full-size quilts can also be used for miniatures. One of the most useful is called chain-piecing. This method of machine piecing involves making a few blocks at a time. As you sew each seam, rather than cutting the threads at the end, you merely lift the presser foot of the machine and place the next block in place. When all the seams are sewn, the blocks look rather like festival bunting. Snip the joining threads and continue sewing as usual.

Chain-piecing

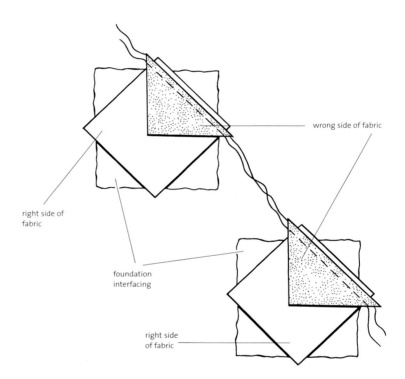

wrong side of fabric

right side of fabric

foundation interfacing

right side of fabric

SUMMARY
- Draw accurate foundations
- Use a fine needle, whether sewing by hand or machine
- Use small stitches, 16 to the inch if possible (stitch length 1.5mm on a sewing machine)
- Start and finish each seam two or three stitches beyond the line so that the seam will not come undone
- Trim all your seam allowances to ⅛in (3mm)
- Press after sewing on each piece of fabric
- Sew a number of blocks at a time
- Work slowly and take frequent breaks

FINISHING YOUR QUILT

arranging blocks

Once you have made all the blocks for a quilt, you need to create a pleasing arrangement and ensure that any dominant fabric is spread evenly across the quilt. For instance, if you have made a blue quilt with a little acid green in it, the green fabric should appear in different parts of the quilt, so that the eye moves over the surface of the quilt, rather than being drawn to one spot. Look at the Black and White Triangles quilt on page 87 – the tiny amounts of red have been arranged to form an irregular triangle. You will find your eye drawn to each of the red hearts, so that you notice more of the quilt than you would if red fabric had only appeared in the centre of the quilt.

Bright heart blocks pinned to corkboard

One advantage of miniature quilts is that it is easy to stand far enough back from the quilt to see the whole design. It can help to squint a little at the blocks to see which colours 'leap out' and so may need to be distributed more evenly across the quilt. I often leave the blocks for a day or two before sewing them together, because I like to look at the quilt with fresh eyes before committing myself to the arrangement.

I find it helpful to use a good quality corkboard for arranging blocks. Once I am happy with the layout, I can pin all of the blocks onto the board until I am ready to sew them together. Sometimes this is days later, but however long I have to wait, I know the blocks will remain in their carefully arranged positions until then.

joining blocks together

After all the work of sewing the patchwork blocks, it is important to take your time when joining the blocks together. I have ruined more than one little quilt by rushing this stage, and finding my square blocks are not square. Remember that an error of $\frac{1}{12}$in (2mm) equates to 1in (2.5cm) in full-size patchwork, so precision is important.

You may decide to separate the blocks using sashing strips, as I did for the Noah's Ark and Hearts quilts (pages 73 and 117). See page 42 for the section on sashing strips.

To join two blocks together, place them with their right sides together. Make sure you know which seam you are going to sew, then place pins vertically through each corner of the blocks. Reposition the two blocks as necessary until the pins pass through the corners accurately.

Pin the blocks together along the seam you are going to sew, then sew the seam using small stitches. If you enjoy hand sewing, I recommend you sew the blocks together by hand, using a small running stitch. When you reach the end of the seam, turn your work over and sew back along the seam line to make the join secure.

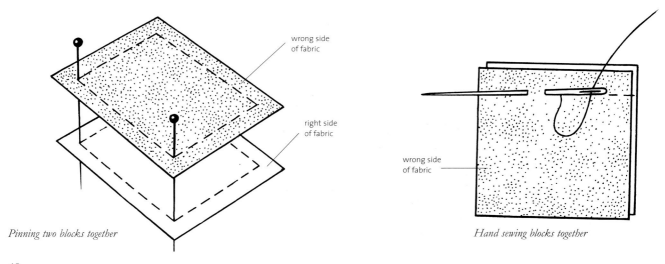

wrong side of fabric

right side of fabric

wrong side of fabric

Pinning two blocks together

Hand sewing blocks together

It is easier to keep on the seam line when sewing by hand than it is when sewing by machine. Having said that, I sew most of my blocks together by machine, unpicking then re-sewing part of a seam where necessary. If you choose to use your sewing machine, work slowly, and take frequent breaks, as it is hard to sew accurately when your eyes are tired.

I choose not to tack (baste) the seams before sewing, because the tacking thread can become caught in the sewing machine. However, I sometimes tack the beginning and end of each seam by hand as this can be more secure than pinning.

When you have joined the blocks together, trim the seam allowance to ⅛in (3mm). Press the seam either open or to one side, depending on where the seams fall in the patchwork blocks. If it is important to press seams in a particular direction, I have given pressing guidelines as part of the project instructions.

I recommend joining blocks together to make strips which run from the top of the bed to the bottom. This allows the quilt to drape better over the sides of the bed, because there is usually a long seam at the side where the quilt can fold. These strips can then be sewn together to make the quilt top.

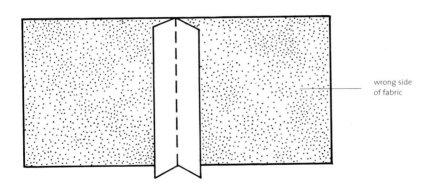

Pressing joining seams open

wrong side
of fabric

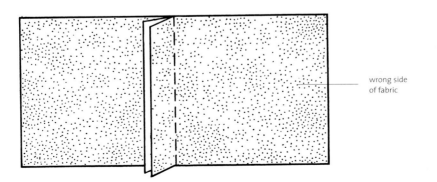

Pressing joining seams to one side

wrong side
of fabric

41

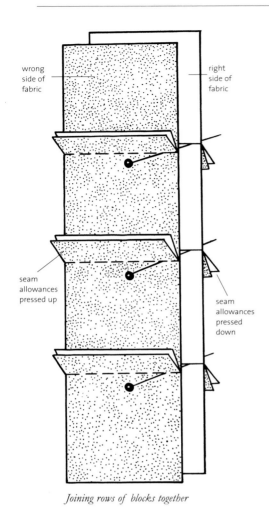

wrong side of fabric

right side of fabric

seam allowances pressed up

seam allowances pressed down

Joining rows of blocks together

Join your rows of blocks together, matching the corners of the blocks. To do this, pass a pin vertically through the corners of the blocks, moving the strips of blocks carefully until the corners all match. Pin and sew these long joining seams either by hand or by machine.

sashing strips

The purpose of sashing strips is to give more space between the patchwork blocks, which produces a calmer quilt. When I was making the Noah's Ark quilt on page 73, I selected various animal-print fabrics, and made a few sample blocks with different sashing fabrics. The brown sashing on this little quilt makes a series of 'windows', with different animals looking out.

There are two other quilts in this book which use sashing strips all around each block – the Hearts quilt on page 117 and Tropical Fish on page 103. In both cases, the motifs would be squashed against each other without the sashing strips, making the quilt busier and the shapes hard to see. The Flying Geese quilt on page 127 only uses sashing strips running down the quilt, which separate the rows of 'geese'.

So, how do you include sashing strips in a quilt? The first step is to decide how wide to make the strips. Using the Hearts quilt as an example, we will explore the effect of altering the width of sashing strips. The heart block is just over ¾in (2cm) square, and I made 49 blocks, which were sewn together in seven rows of seven. If there had been no sashing strips, the quilt top would have measured 5½in (14cm) before binding. Since this is too small for most beds, I would have to make the hearts larger or make more of them to end up with a quilt 8in (20cm) square.

One significant advantage of putting sashing strips between patchwork blocks is that you can easily alter the width of the strips and so make a quilt which will fit your bed perfectly. The table below shows the effect of different widths of sashing strips. Since there are seven hearts, you need eight sashing strips – six between the hearts, and one on either side of the quilt.

Total size of heart blocks	Size of sashing strips		Finished size of quilt top
	Each strip	Total	
5½in (14cm)	⅛in (3mm)	1in (2.5cm)	6½in (16.5cm)
5½in (14cm)	3⁄16in (4.5mm)	1½in (3.8cm)	7in (17.7cm)
5½in (14cm)	¼in (6mm)	2in (5cm)	7½in (19cm)

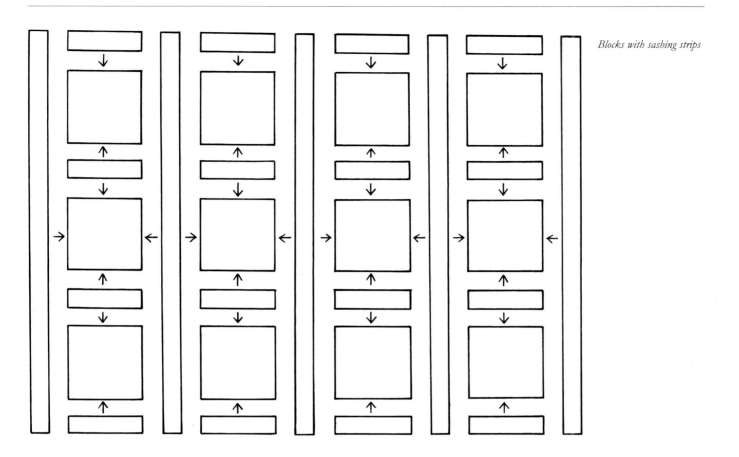

Blocks with sashing strips

In the table opposite, notice how the size of each sashing strip increases only slightly – 1⁄8in to 3⁄16in to 1⁄4in (3mm to 4.5mm to 6mm) – yet the overall size of the quilt grows much more quickly. Choose the width which results in a quilt to fit your bed.

Now that you have decided on the width of your sashing strips, you need to cut them and sew them onto the blocks. If you know before you begin sewing that you will use sashing strips, you can draw the foundation patterns to include them. I did this for the Hearts quilt on page 117, which has sashing strips included at the top of each heart motif. If this is the case, just sew the sashing strips onto the blocks in the normal way.

However, if you decide to use sashing strips after making your patchwork blocks, you will need to cut them out carefully from your chosen fabric. This is one time when I find a rotary cutter and cutting mat very useful. If you are not familiar with using a rotary cutter, try borrowing one from a friend. The main points to remember are:

• Make sure the fabric you plan to cut has been ironed so there are no creases in it
• Find the straight grain of the fabric, and cut along this to give a neat edge. It is often easier to see the grain on the wrong side of printed fabric
• Line up the cut edge of the fabric along one of the straight lines on the cutting mat

- Make the sashing strips approximately ½in (12mm) wider than the required finished width
- Lay a quilter's rule parallel with the cut edge, the correct distance from the edge (the lines printed on the cutting mat and on the ruler are useful for measuring the distance)
- Press down firmly with the ruler to ensure that the fabric cannot move while you are cutting it
- Cut smoothly with the rotary cutter, pressing the blade lightly against the ruler as you cut

Sew the blocks together into long rows, with narrow sashing strips between each block. Joining the sashing strip onto the first block is not difficult – just make sure that you keep the fabric straight. It is a little trickier to sew on the next block. Pin the second block onto the sashing fabric, making sure that the blocks will line up neatly when they are all sewn together. I often use the patchwork foot on my sewing machine as a guide, since I know that this gives a ¼in (6mm) seam allowance. By guiding the edge of the sewing machine foot against the seam which joins the sashing strip to the first patchwork block, I know that the sashing will end up ¼in (6mm) wide.

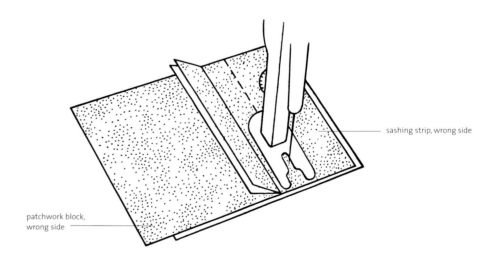

Guide the sewing machine foot along the first seam, to give a constant ¼in (6mm) sashing strip

sashing strip, wrong side

patchwork block, wrong side

If you are sewing by hand, use a quilter's quarter-inch rule to draw a line to sew along (see panel on facing page). Alternatively you could try using the narrow marking tape which some quilting shops sell, as a temporary guide.

When the blocks are joined into rows, you can attach long sashing strips to the edge. Again, cut these with a rotary cutter if possible to give accurate strips. Sew on carefully, and join the rows together. It is best to pin in a few places along the seams, so that the sides of the quilt will end up straight. Sew slowly and carefully, then press the seam allowance towards the sashing strips.

HINT

Quilting shops sell a special ruler called a 'quilter's quarter-inch rule'. This is a clear plastic ruler which is exactly ¼in (6mm) wide. For strength, it is a square section ruler, that is, the ruler is ¼in (6mm) high as well as wide. I sometimes place my quilter's rule against the seam joining a sashing strip to a patchwork block, and draw a light pencil line on the wrong side of the sashing strip. This gives me a line to sew along, exactly ¼in (6mm) from the first seam.

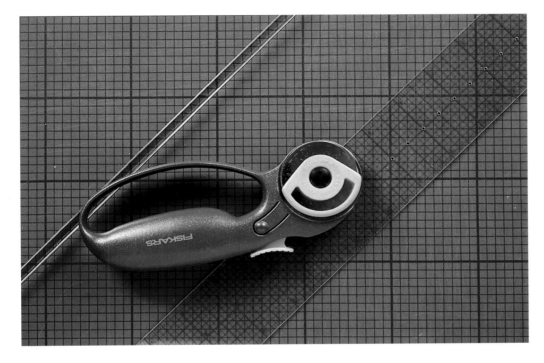

Cutting mat, with, from left to right: quilter's quarter-inch rule, rotary cutter and quilter's rule

borders

When all the patchwork blocks have been made and joined together, you are ready to turn the quilt top into a real quilt. The main steps involved are borders, quilting and binding.

Many of my quilts do not have borders. Instead, the whole quilt is made up of patchwork blocks, and I add a narrow binding to finish the quilt. Sometimes, though, a quilt looks much better with a border.

In its simplest form, a border can be just a narrow strip of fabric in a contrasting colour sewn on before the binding is added. The Red Log Cabin quilt on page 91 and the Hearts quilt on page 117 both have narrow borders, one cream and the other dark pink. Occasionally, despite all your careful measuring and sewing, a quilt may be slightly too short for the bed. Adding a narrow border is an excellent way of sorting out this problem.

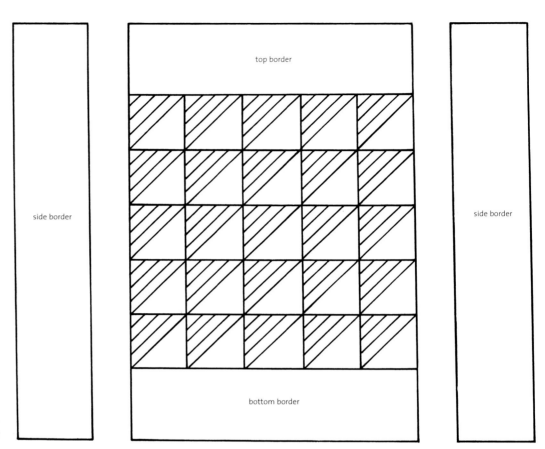

Adding square-cornered borders

Wide borders with hand quilting are a feature of Amish quilts, so the quilt on page 107 has borders 1in (2.5cm) wide. The Lighthouse and Boats quilt on page 139 has a more complex border which frames the central design like a picture, while Blue Windmills on page 123 and Riotous Pennants on page 111 also have dramatic borders.

There are two different ways of dealing with the corners when you add a border:

Squared corners

The first is to add border strips to the top and bottom of the quilt, then sew on the side borders. This is the easier approach, and is perfectly acceptable when you are using plain fabric, so the Red Log Cabin, Hearts and Amish-style quilts all use this method.

To add a square-cornered border, cut strips of fabric using a rotary cutter (see sashing strips section, pages 43–4, for guidance) the width of the border plus ½in (12mm). Sew the top and bottom borders in place, trim the seams and press well. Now add the side borders in the same way.

Mitred borders

The second, more complicated approach to borders, is to mitre the corners. This

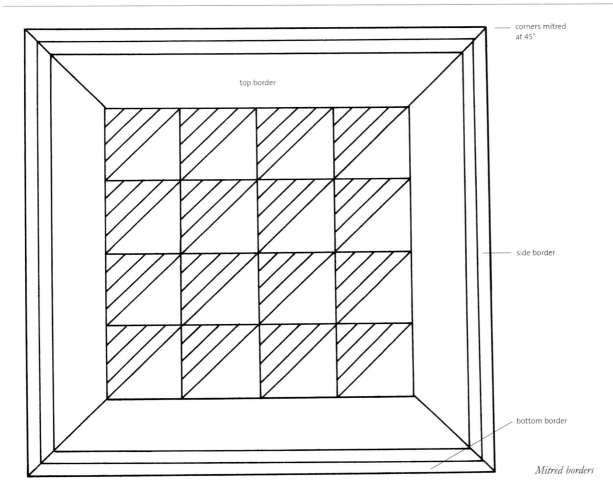

corners mitred
at 45°

top border

side border

bottom border

Mitred borders

means to sew the side borders to the top and bottom borders using a 45° seam. I used this approach on the Blue Windmills quilt and the Lighthouse and Boats quilt (see pages 123 and 139). Mitred borders are particularly effective where more than one fabric is used in the border.

Mitred borders use more fabric than squared corners, and are more complicated to sew. If you plan to try them, be prepared to have to unpick the corner seam a little and re-sew it.

Make the border following the instructions given for the quilt. Make sure that all of the borders are a little longer than the finished size of the quilt. For example, for a quilt 8in (20cm) square, make your borders 8½in (21.2cm) long.

Sew the top and bottom borders in place, starting and stopping exactly ¼in (6mm) from the edges. Finish your seams so they cannot unravel. Now sew the side borders in place, stopping at the same place in the corners.

Next, fold your quilt in half on the diagonal. Move the quilt carefully until one of the side borders and the bottom border are on top of each other, with their edges aligned.

Place a ruler on top of the quilt, and draw a light pencil line on the border, continuing the diagonal line.

Marking mitred corners

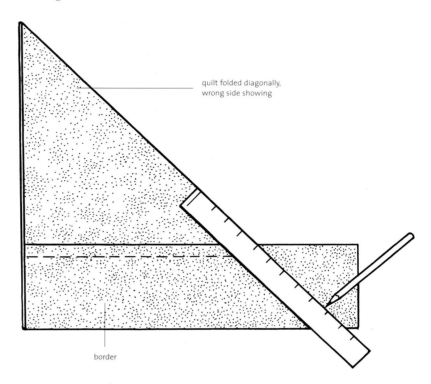

quilt folded diagonally, wrong side showing

border

Pin very carefully along this line, then open the borders out and check that the quilt lies flat. When you are happy with the position of the pins, sew this seam. Repeat for the other three corners.

quilting

Quilting started as a practical way of joining the three layers of a quilt together, but has developed into an art form. Many full-scale quilts include beautiful, detailed quilting, which adds enormously to the final quilt. However, I have found that it is best to keep the quilting quite simple for dolls' house quilts.

First lay out the completed quilt top, the wadding and the backing fabric on a flat surface. Make sure the backing fabric has been ironed well and is not creased. Choose a lightweight fabric for the backing, such as silk or cotton lawn, and try to use a patterned fabric, as this hides the quilting stitches. The wadding and the backing fabric should extend about 1in (2.5cm) all round the quilt top.

Pin carefully around the outside of the quilt, catching all three layers together. If you plan to use hand quilting, I suggest you add a few extra pins at the corners of some of the blocks and tack (baste) around the outside of the quilt, as it is important that the layers all stay in the same place as you quilt.

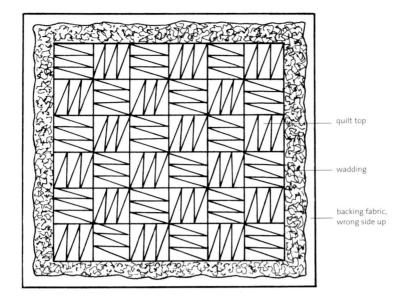

Quilt top, wadding and backing fabric

quilt top

wadding

backing fabric, wrong side up

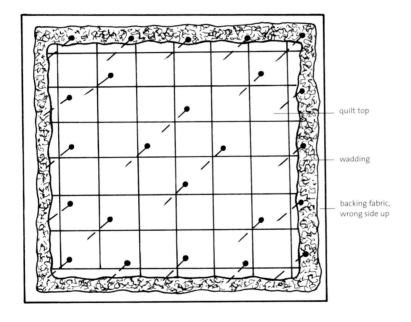

Pin the three layers together at seam intersections

quilt top

wadding

backing fabric, wrong side up

If you will be using a sewing machine with a walking foot for the quilting, you may not need to use many pins to keep everything together.

You have a number of decisions to make before you start quilting. Will you sew by hand or machine? Do you want your quilting stitches to be seen? Which parts of the patchwork design do you want to emphasize?

In each quilt project I explain what sort of quilting I have used and this will give you an idea of the effect of each approach. For examples of hand quilting designed to be seen, look at Appliqué Hearts and Amish-style Roman Stripes on pages 95 and 107. For invisible hand quilting, see Red Log Cabin and Peach Ninepatch on pages 91 and 135. Some of the quilts have machine quilting which just echoes the patchwork shape, such as Hearts and Tropical Fish on pages 117 and 103. In other quilts, the machine quilting really adds to the overall effect, especially in Stars and Autumn Leaves on pages 145 and 155.

Hand quilting

The biggest challenge in hand quilting is to sew small, even stitches. This is true for full-scale quilting, but especially true for miniature quilts. If you plan to make a feature of the hand quilting, choose a simple motif such as a heart or flower.

With all quilting it is best to work from the centre of the quilt to the outside. This reduces the chance of puckering on the top or the back of the quilt. If you are hand quilting between the patchwork blocks, and it is possible to sew from one side of the quilt to the other, start with a seam at the middle of the quilt. Use a length of fine cotton or cotton/polyester thread about 12in (30cm) long. Make two small stitches very near the edge of the quilt, to secure the thread where the binding will later cover them. Using tiny stitches, sew through all layers of the quilt.

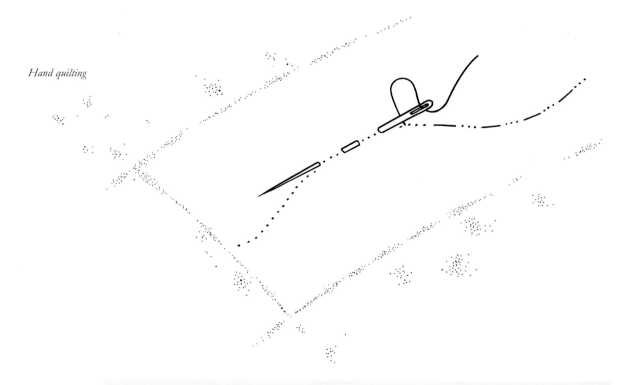

Hand quilting

> **HINT**
> **When hand quilting, it is easier to sew a curved shape, such as a heart, than to sew straight lines, as it is less obvious if your stitches are a little askew.**

If possible, take two or three stitches on the needle before pulling the thread through. This will produce more even stitches than sewing each one individually. As you sew over seam allowances, however, this will not be possible. The alternative is to use stab stitching, where the needle passes directly through the layers of fabric to the bottom, then back through to the top. Rather than sewing a stitch in one smooth motion, stab stitching is two separate actions for each stitch.

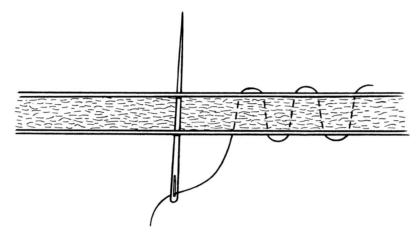

Stab stitching

If your quilting takes you to the other side of the quilt, just finish off the thread with two small stitches and cut the thread.

Often you will be sewing individual motifs, so will need to mark the design on the quilt top before quilting. While there are many marking pens available, I am reluctant to use them for 1/12 scale quilts. Your quilts will be studied closely, and any remaining quilting mark will be seen. I prefer to cut the shapes from paper and stick them in place with a small piece of double-sided sticky tape, or cut motifs from freezer paper and iron these onto the quilt.

When you have sewn around one motif you can finish off the thread and start again on another part of the quilt. Or you can pass the needle through the wadding layer to the next section of the quilt, but make sure your needle doesn't go through the backing fabric.

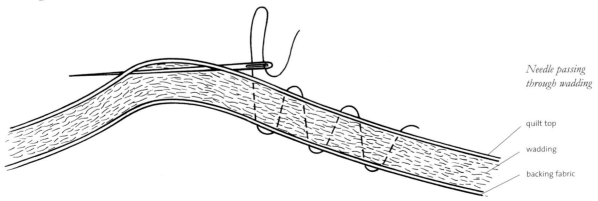

Needle passing through wadding

quilt top

wadding

backing fabric

Although hand quilting is time consuming, the results can be stunning. I recommend practising your quilting stitches on some spare fabric until you are completely happy with the results.

Machine quilting

Machine quilting is generally quicker than hand quilting and gives a more solid outline. Since it is difficult to quilt over seam allowances, it is best to use machine quilting in areas of the quilt with few seams. You can choose to outline a patchwork shape by sewing very close to the seams, or machine quilt in open border areas.

If you have a walking foot (even-feed foot) for your sewing machine, try using it for machine quilting. You will be amazed at the difference it makes. Because the fabric is fed through the presser foot from above as well as from below, the three layers of the quilt stay together beautifully. I have even quilted some of these quilts without pinning the layers together at all, using my walking foot.

Machine quilting to outline shapes

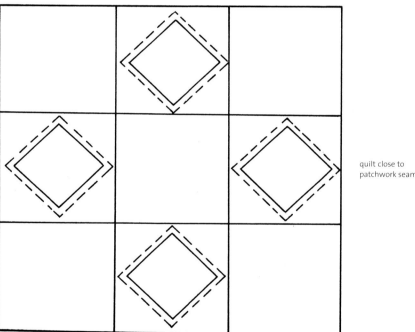

quilt close to patchwork seams

As with hand quilting, start near the middle of the quilt. Sew slowly and carefully, finishing with the needle down in the fabric if your sewing machine has this option. Lift the presser foot and move the quilt to turn corners. I find it difficult to sew curves on my sewing machine, so prefer to choose designs with straight lines.

You may find that you have to start and stop often, and that you end up with lots of loose ends of thread. When you have finished quilting, pull the front thread through

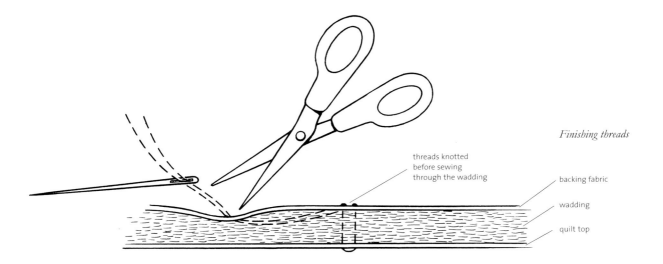

Finishing threads

threads knotted
before sewing
through the wadding

backing fabric

wadding

quilt top

to the back of the quilt and tie a double knot. Thread a needle with the loose ends of thread, and take a stitch just into the wadding layer of the quilt. If you pull the thread taut before you snip it, the end should disappear into the quilt.

buttons and beads

On two of the quilts in this book – Country Squares and Kaleidoscope, on pages 69 and 151 – I used buttons or beads instead of quilting to join the layers together. To do this, layer the quilt top, wadding and backing fabric as already explained, then pin around the outside of the quilt to keep the layers together. Starting near the middle of the quilt where you want the first bead or button to go, sew two or three small stitches on top of each other to make the thread secure. Pass the needle through all three layers from the quilt top to the backing fabric, then bring the needle back up to the quilt top, very close to where the stitch started. You will have to use stab stitches, since you will be passing the needle through seam allowances.

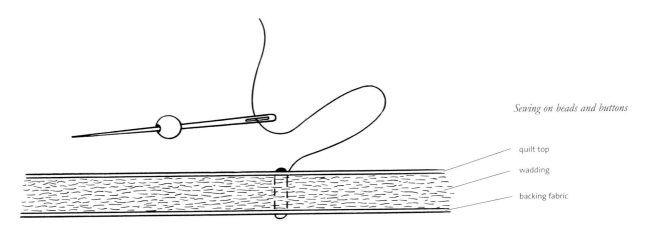

Sewing on beads and buttons

quilt top

wadding

backing fabric

Pass the needle through the bead or button, then back through the quilt 'sandwich'. Fasten off the thread on the back of the quilt, then snip off the thread. Keep adding buttons or beads, working from the centre of the quilt to the outside. Each time you start sewing in a new place, check that the backing fabric is not becoming creased.

binding

After quilting, the final step is to sew a binding around the outside of the quilt to finish off the edges. Most of the time I have used the main fabric of the quilt, or one of the fabrics from the patchwork blocks, so that the binding does not detract from the patchwork. There are two exceptions: Autumn Leaves on page 155, where I used the leaf-patterned fabric that inspired the quilt, and the Amish-style quilt on page 107. Amish quilts often have a contrasting binding, so I chose bright blue which looks lovely against the grey border.

With a rectangular quilt you have the choice of binding strips cut on the straight grain, or cut on the bias. If you are new to quilt making, I would recommend using straight-grain strips, moving to bias strips as you become more confident. The method I like to use involves folding the binding in half, so that you have a fold of fabric to sew down on the wrong side of the quilt. Whether you choose bias strips or straight-grain binding, you will need a rectangle of fabric approximately 6 × 10in (15 × 25cm).

Straight-grain binding

It is best to measure the finished size of your quilt across the middle of the quilt, because the edges sometimes stretch a little. Add 1in (2.5cm) to give you the length of the binding strips. Decide how wide you wish the binding to be – mine are usually ¼in (6mm) wide, though occasionally I make them narrower. Multiply the width by six. So, for a ¼in (6mm) binding you start with fabric strips 1½in (3.8cm) wide. You need to cut four binding strips, ideally with a rotary cutter, so that the strips are an even width.

Fold the binding strips in half lengthways, and press well. Starting with the sides of the quilt, pin the binding in place along the edge, with ½in (12mm) of the binding sticking out at either end. You will need to pin the binding in a few places. Sew carefully into place, either by hand or machine, then press lightly, taking care not to press the quilting area of your quilt. Using a rotary cutter, trim the side edges of the quilt so that the seam allowance is just under ¼in (6mm).

Turn the binding to the wrong side of the quilt and sew into place by hand, using small stitches. You are aiming to cover the previous line of stitching, to give a neat back on the quilt. If necessary, trim the seam allowances a little more, so that the binding will cover the stitches when it is folded to the back. Trim the extra ½in (12mm) off at each end.

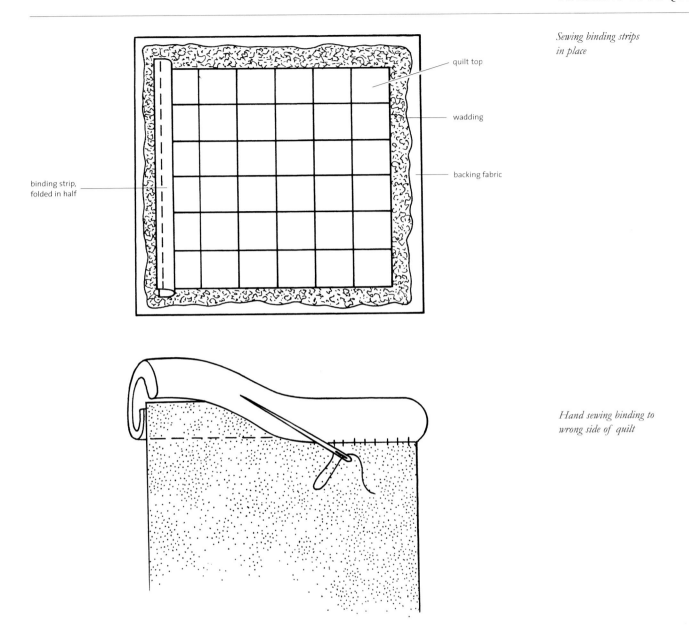

quilt top

wadding

backing fabric

binding strip, folded in half

Now attach binding strips to the top and bottom of the quilt in the same way. This time you will need to fold the extra ½in (12mm) of the binding over and sew down neatly to finish the corners.

Bias binding

Some quilters prefer to use bias strips for the binding, which can give neater corners on the quilt. To make bias-binding strips, take a rectangle of fabric 6 × 10in (15 × 25cm) and press it well to remove creases. Place the fabric on a cutting board and measure carefully 6in (15cm) from the bottom left corner. Mark this position accurately with a pin or tailor's chalk, then place your quilter's rule across the fabric to join this mark to the top left corner. Cut along the ruler, giving a 45° cut. Now cut binding strips parallel with this bias edge, four times wider than the finished width of your binding. For example, ¼in (6mm) binding will require bias strips cut 1in (2.5cm) wide.

Cutting bias-binding strips

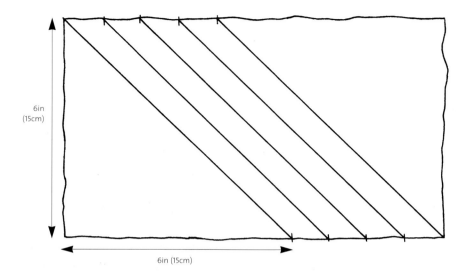

6in (15cm)

6in (15cm)

The hardest part of using bias strips is joining them together to make a continuous strip long enough to go all the way around the quilt. Place two binding strips together as shown, then sew the joining seam and press it flat.

When you sew bias binding around a quilt, start halfway along the bottom of the quilt. Turn the end of the binding to the wrong side before you start, then sew the binding all the way round the quilt. Use the edge of the presser foot on your sewing machine to help you sew ¼in (6mm) from the edge of the quilt. Or, if you are sewing by hand, draw a faint pencil line ¼in (6mm) from the edge of the binding as a guide.

Sewing bias strips together

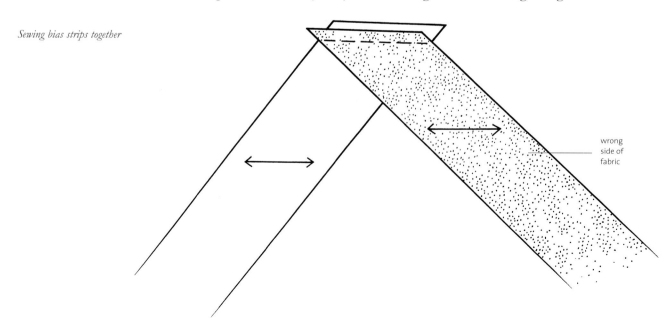

wrong side of fabric

On full-sized quilts, bias bindings often have mitred corners, but I find this to be too bulky on dolls' house quilts. I prefer just to round the corner off slightly as I sew.

Press the binding gently towards the edge of the quilt, then press under ¼in (6mm) on the other edge of the binding. Trim the seam allowances a little, then sew the binding in place on the wrong side of the quilt using small stitches.

beds with footposts

If your quilt is not rectangular, that is, it has been made to fit a bed with footposts, you will need to use straight-grain strips of fabric for the binding. Start by sewing the binding in the L-shaped sections at the foot of the bed. To do this, open out the L-shape until it is a straight line, snipping the seam allowance to make it open out. Sew a short binding strip in place, making sure you sew right into the corner.

Hand sew the binding in place on the back of the quilt, then add a binding to the bottom and sides of the quilt. Finish with a binding strip along the top of the quilt.

using florists' wire

To make the quilt sit well on a bed, you may wish to use florists' wire sewn into the binding. I use two pieces of fine wire, twisted together. When I have sewn the binding onto the quilt, but before I hand sew it in place on the back, I sew the wire into the seam allowance. Every few stitches I push my needle between the two strands of wire, so that it stays in the correct place.

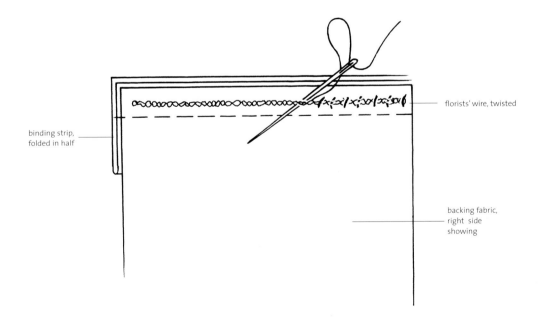

Sewing florists' wire into binding

florists' wire, twisted

binding strip, folded in half

backing fabric, right side showing

Trim the wire so that it is a little shorter than the binding, then finish sewing the binding in place.

labels

Now that your miniature quilt is finished, you should consider adding a label to the back of the quilt. I have fabric name-tape labels which say 'Designed and Made by Sarah Williams', which is a neat option for such small quilts. You could try writing your initials or name and the date on a scrap of fabric, and sewing this in place. Some people write directly onto the back of their quilts using a permanent fabric pen, while others embroider their details. Whatever method you choose, it is worth labelling your creation.

positioning the quilt on the bed

The final step is to put the quilt on the bed, and make sure that it stays in place. Some quilts sit very well on a bed, while others need a little assistance. Start by putting the quilt on the bed, and smooth it into place. If the quilt has wire in the top and/or bottom binding, bend this to the shape of the bed. Otherwise, leave the quilt on the bed for a day or two as quilts often 'relax' into the shape of the bed.

If the quilt is still sticking out a little from the bed, press the quilt gently with your fingers along the sides of the bed to help it fit the shape. I sometimes use a very light steam from my iron to relax the fabric (but be careful if you have printed your foundation patterns on a computer, as the quilt must not get too wet). For a bed with footposts, a small stitch joining the side and bottom borders together behind the footposts can hold a quilt in place. If all else fails, you can use a little double-sided sticky tape to attach the quilt to the bed.

USING A COMPUTER

I have designed most of the quilts in this book using my computer. In this chapter I explain the advantages of using a computer to produce patchwork foundations, as well as some of the problems I have encountered with this process. If you have no interest in computers, and especially if you plan only to make the more simple quilts in this book, there is no need to read the instructions I give here.

advantages of using a computer

There are a number of advantages to producing patchwork foundations by computer:

- The printed blocks are more accurate than hand-drawn blocks, because the printed lines are thinner than pencil lines
- All the blocks are exactly the same size, which gives a more accurate result
- It can be hard to draw pencil lines on interfacing without ripping the interfacing, so printing the foundations is easier
- The size of a patchwork block can be changed easily, so that the quilt will fit each bed perfectly
- If you decide to make the same quilt again in another colourway, you need only print out the blocks, which is much quicker than drawing them by hand

Of course, drawing the design on the computer takes some time, so you have to weigh up whether the time saved in producing the foundation patterns warrants the time spent drawing the block on the computer. Many of the easier quilts at the beginning of the book can be produced accurately without using a computer. However, the more complex quilts such as Autumn Leaves and Kaleidoscope on pages 155 and 151 do require the computer-drawn foundations.

If you do not own a computer, or your computer skills are limited, perhaps you have a friend or family member who could do this for you? Many teenagers would be happy to earn a little extra pocket money, while also showing off their superior knowledge!

Quilting software

There are some excellent software packages on the market which can produce quilt designs and print foundation papers. I have not used any of them, so cannot comment on which is the most useful for dolls' house patchwork – you will need to look at recent issues of quilting magazines for reviews, or contact the software manufacturers with your questions.

I produced all of the designs in this book using a word-processing package which has some drawing tools. All you need is the ability to draw simple shapes, such as squares, triangles and lines, and to be able to move them and re-size them.

If your computer has a word-processing or drawing package, have a look to see what it can do. You do not necessarily need the latest version of software – indeed, in computer terms, the software I use is old-fashioned at best.

Since each software package is different, I cannot give detailed instructions on how to reproduce these patchwork designs. However, I can give some general guidelines which should help you.

If you haven't worked through a tutorial for your word processor, this is a good place to start. You can probably skip some of the sections, and look just at drawing shapes.

Many bookshops sell 'how to' books specific to different software packages, or your local library may have one. See if there is one that covers drawing shapes.

Drawing tools may not appear automatically when you go into a word-processing package. You may need to tell the computer to display them – check out the toolbars to see if there is one for drawing shapes.

Worked example – triangles quilt

Try working through this example to check that you know enough about drawing objects to start producing foundation patterns. I have assumed that you are familiar with the computer mouse and the basic functions of the word processor.

1in (2.5cm) square

Start by drawing a 1in (2.5cm) square. This may appear initially as a rectangle rather than a square but you can alter the size of a shape to make it square. Look for Format Object or Format Autoshape, then find the size section. Change both the height and width to 1in (or 2.5cm if your computer uses metric measurements).

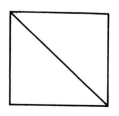

1in (2.5cm) square plus diagonal

Add a diagonal line from the top left corner to the bottom right, which will split the square and make two triangles. It can be hard to start and stop a line accurately in the corner of a square. Try using Zoom to make the square appear bigger on the screen. Whenever I am trying to place lines accurately, I zoom to 200% or larger so that errors appear enormous. These can then be corrected, and when you return to normal size, the block will look perfect.

Draw two more lines parallel with the diagonal, on either side.

When you are happy with the placement of these lines, click on the diagonal and delete it. You will then be left with the pattern for the Black and White Triangles quilt which is shown on page 88.

The next step is to select all parts of the design, that is the original square plus the two lines. You may need to click on a special pointer to be able to select the shape. Find out how to Group the square and the lines, so that you can treat it as one object, rather than separate pieces. Grouping may appear as part of the drawing toolbar.

Now you need to find out how to copy the block. This will often be part of the Edit section of the software. Select the block, Copy it then Paste it. If you keep clicking on Paste, you will get multiple copies. Try and make a row of blocks and use Zoom to get an accurate view of what you are doing.

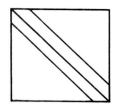

1in (2.5cm) square plus three diagonal lines

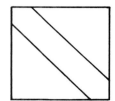

Triangles pattern

 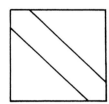 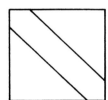 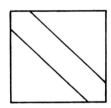 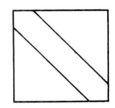

A row of templates

When you wish to print out templates for patchwork, the square blocks will need to be about ½in apart (1.2cm), so that you are able to cut the foundation interfacing into separate blocks.

It can be useful to fill a page with your chosen block without any gaps in between, and print this out. You can then colour it in to see the effect of using different colours in the quilt. You may need to rotate or flip the block to see how it will look in a finished quilt. These features are also useful when you are drawing blocks made in two halves, such as for Autumn Leaves on page 155.

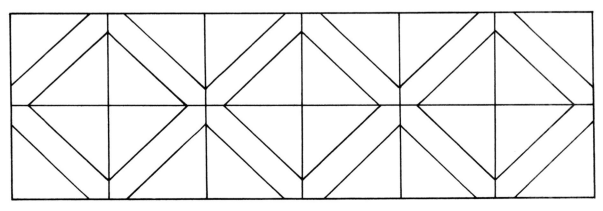

Templates close together

If you start with a square and draw the pattern only using lines, you should have a clear design to print out. Sometimes, however, you will need to use triangles or rectangles inside the square block. You may find that a new shape partially obscures a shape you drew earlier. If this is the case, check the Fill Colour of the new shape. Often, a word-processor draws white shapes, where you really want just the outline of a shape. Change the Fill Colour to No Fill, and you should be able to see all the lines again.

Scanning

If you have access to a scanner, you could scan in the patterns from this book, rather than drawing them yourself. Although the quality of the printed lines is not quite as good from a scanned image as from a computer-drawn one, they are still much more accurate than hand-drawn patterns. Also, it is much faster to scan an image than to use a computer drawing package. You will probably need to alter the size of the scanned image using Format Object or Format Autoshape in your word-processing software, to make sure that it is the correct size.

Printing

When you have drawn or scanned your pattern, and copied it to fill the page, you are ready to print it out. I strongly recommend printing out onto plain paper first, so that you can check that the pattern is the correct size. You should also check that you have left sufficient space between the foundation blocks, so that they can be cut apart for sewing.

Over the course of writing this book, I have used two different printers for producing foundation patterns. Because they handle paper differently, the method I had developed for printing foundations on one printer did not work on the second. However, that means I can offer you two different techniques, and I hope that at least one will work for your printer.

Method One
You will need:
- Sheet of plain paper to fit your printer (A4 or letter size)
- Fine interfacing cut to the same width, but 1in (2.5cm) longer
- Double-sided sticky tape

1. Attach a strip of double-sided sticky tape near the top of the sheet of paper
2. Lay the paper on top of the interfacing, with the sticky tape facing up, and the extra length of interfacing visible
3. Fold the extra interfacing over the top edge of the A4 paper, and stick it down. Press firmly along the top edge to form a crease, but do not iron it, as this would distort the paper too much, and the printer would probably jam

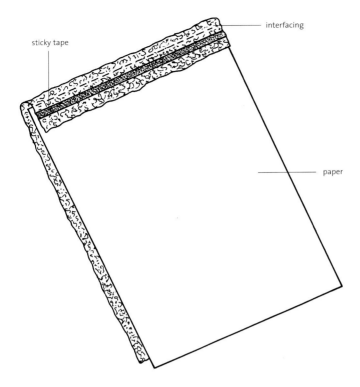

sticky tape

interfacing

paper

*Joining paper and
interfacing for printing*

Method Two

You will need:

- ♦ Freezer paper, cut to the correct size for your printer (A4 or letter size)
- ♦ Fine interfacing cut to the same size

Iron the freezer paper onto the interfacing, making sure that the two layers are securely joined around all the edges.

Now you will need to experiment a little with your printer. Check whether paper needs to be face up or face down as it enters the printer. Either read the instruction manual, or do a print test by writing 'front' and 'back' on a piece of paper and seeing which side is printed on.

Sheets of paper with interfacing attached will need to be fed one at a time through the printer. I found that the printing was no problem with my basic printer, but the interfacing often jammed in the printer as it came out. I was able to open up the front of my printer and guide the pattern sheet out gently as it printed.

> **HINT**
> Freezer paper is available in supermarkets in the USA, and in some quilting shops in other countries. It has a thick wax coating on one side, which melts when the paper is ironed. When the paper cools, it sticks to the interfacing or fabric.

For each quilt, you will need either one or two pages of patterns. When you have printed out the foundations, remove them from the paper or freezer paper, taking care not to stretch or tear the interfacing. I have found that freezer paper should be removed straight away, or it sticks too well to the interfacing. If this happens to you, try ironing the freezer paper with a warm iron to melt the wax and free the interfacing.

size of pattern

When you have printed your pattern out onto the interfacing, please check the size again carefully. When I used the first method (attaching interfacing to plain paper with double-sided sticky tape) I found that the interfacing separated a little from the paper while printing, which resulted in the pattern being too short. I compensated for this by making all of my patterns 4% longer than the required size. Your printer may require a slightly different adjustment to the length. I did not have the same problem using freezer paper ironed onto the interfacing.

disadvantages of inkjet printers

The main disadvantage of using an inkjet printer to produce the patterns for quilts is that the ink used is not permanent. It does not matter if the ink fades in time, as the foundation interfacing is hidden inside the finished quilt. However, if you have an inkjet printer you will know that the ink runs if it gets wet. So the finished quilt cannot be washed, and you need to be careful to use a dry iron rather than a steam iron when pressing the pieces. In practice I have found that I can use a little bit of steam, but not a water spray or heavy steam.

There is a product available which you can use to make inkjet printing permanent. However, it was designed for printing quilt labels, and requires the fabric to be soaked in the solution before quilting. If you anticipate wanting to wash the finished quilt, I would suggest trying this out.

Printer manufacturers are starting to produce permanent, archival quality inks for inkjet printers. So, if you are buying a new printer it is worth checking to see whether the ink will be waterproof.

You may have access to a laser printer, in which case it would be worth experimenting with it. Laser printer inks are permanent, and do not run when wet. Be aware, however, that the paper often passes through a complex route within a laser printer, so the interfacing may tear or become jammed. The same applies to photocopiers – the ink is permanent, however the interfacing may become jammed inside the machine. You will also need to check that your foundation patterns are the correct size, as laser printers and photocopiers sometimes distort the image a little.

the
QUILT PROJECTS

This section of the book contains twenty different quilts for you to make. I have arranged them in order of difficulty, so that the easier quilts appear first and the more complex designs near the end. Any of the quilts can be altered to fit a different size of bed, or can be made in another colour scheme to suit your dolls' house.

Before you start reading about making patchwork quilts in 1/12 scale, you might like to consider an even easier way to make dolls' house quilts. If you look carefully in patchwork shops, you may find fabrics which are printed to look like miniature quilts, or which make convincing quilts without much work. If you can find a suitable fabric, all you need to do is cut it to the correct size then layer it with some lightweight wadding and a backing fabric. Add some quilting and a narrow binding to finish.

I found some more ideas for simulated patchwork quilts in *Miniature Embroidery for the Victorian Dolls' House* by Pamela Warner (GMC Publications), which also contains many other lovely projects.

quilt 1 COUNTRY SQUARES

This is the easiest quilt to make, as there is very little sewing and no quilting, yet it is really effective, and would make any cottage bedroom look cosy and inviting.

The quilt only needs very small pieces of fabric, so I mainly used fabric swatches from a mail order company. Part of the quilt's charm is that all the fabric blocks are different, so it is worth finding 64 suitable fabrics if you can. I chose earthy colours, and included a number of stripes and checks, which add to the country feel. If you look closely, you will see a watering can and a bee, as well as one print which reminds me of chickens' feet!

I designed this quilt to fit on a simple wooden bed with no footboard or footposts. Altering the pattern to fit your dolls' house bed is straightforward, since the blocks can be a little larger or smaller than the 1in (2.5cm) squares I have used (see page 14 for instructions).

1 Either draw eight copies of the Country Squares template on fine, sew-in interfacing, or draw accurate 1in (2.5cm) squares on the wrong side of the fabric with a sharp pencil. This is much easier to do if you draw around a metal template. Metal templates are sold by many craft and patchwork shops, but you could make your own out of cardboard, using the template on page 70 as a guide.

MATERIALS

- Assortment of brown, cream and green fabrics, each 1½in (3.8cm) square
- Brown fabric for binding, 10 × 6in (25 × 15cm)
- Optional: Fine, sew-in interfacing, 8 × 12in (20 × 30cm)
- 1in (2.5cm) square template (shop-bought or home-made – see stage 1)
- Lightweight wadding, 10in (25cm) square
- Backing fabric, 10in (25cm) square
- Matching thread
- 49 tiny buttons or beads (see 'Hint' on page 70)
- Florists' wire

Finished size: 8 × 8in
(20 × 20cm)

Country Squares template (actual size)

HINT

You can make your own buttons from oven-hardening clay. To do this, roll out cream-coloured clay until it is very thin, ideally ¹⁄₁₆in (1.5mm) thick, then cut out tiny circles – I broke a cheap paintbrush and used the ferrule (the metal end that holds the bristles in place) as my cutter.

Before putting the buttons in the oven to harden, make two holes in each one with a needle (don't use your finest needle, as you will need that to sew the buttons onto the quilt). Follow the manufacturer's instructions for baking and allow to cool.

It's a good idea to make more buttons than you will need, as some may break when you sew them on. Don't worry if they are not perfectly round, as that will just add to the charm of this rustic quilt.

2 Arrange your fabrics to give a balanced quilt top, that is, one where the colours are spread evenly across the quilt. I found it helped to separate my 64 fabrics into eight piles – dark brown, mid-brown, dark green, mid-green, red/rust, cream/beige, checks and 'conversational prints'. I then put one fabric from each pile in each row, trying to ensure that each column also had a mix of colours. Inevitably, this process took some time, but the effect was worth the trouble.

3 Sew the blocks together into eight rows, either using the foundation piecing approach (see page 25) or just matching up the drawn lines on the back of the fabric. If you sew by hand, make sure that your stitches are small and even, and that you start and finish each seam with a backstitch.

4 Press the seams to the left on one row and to the right on the next, to make joining the rows together easier.

5 Join the eight rows together, matching the seams at each intersection. Don't worry if some do not match perfectly, as the little buttons will hide any imperfections.

6 Layer the quilt top, wadding and backing fabric together, then pin or tack carefully. I used polyester wadding which has plenty of 'loft' (see 'wadding', page 9), so that the quilt looks especially warm. Rather than quilting, I sewed tiny buttons at the corners of the squares, which seems to draw all the fabric colours and patterns together.

7 To help this quilt sit well on the bed, I cut off the bottom corners at an angle. Bind the quilt following the instructions on page 54 and, if you wish, sew florists' wire into the top binding and the bottom corners (see instructions for this on page 57).

1	
2	
3	
4	
5	
6	
7	
8	

Country Squares fabric piecing sequence.

COLOUR VARIATION

When my daughter Rebecca needed a little quilt for her dolls' bed, I chose lilac, white and silver fabrics, with a little burgundy as an accent. This time I made the blocks 2in (5cm) square and chose spangly beads for the intersections.

quilt 2 NOAH'S ARK

Each year the dolls' house group I belong to makes a new project to display at the annual dolls' house show. In 2001 each member of the group made a room box and my choice was a child's bedroom, with a Noah's Ark mural and various animal toys.

This quilt was originally designed to be part of the room box. However, once I had decorated the room box, I decided that a fish quilt would suit the room better – so I made the Tropical Fish quilt on page 103. Now all I need to do is make a new room box to display this lovely quilt!

1 First measure your dolls' house bed and adjust the pattern to fit (see page 14 for instructions). This quilt is based on squares of animal fabric measuring just under 1in (2.5cm) with sashing strips ⅕in (5mm) wide between each block; this fits a bed approximately 3½ × 5⅝in (8.7 × 14cm). You can alter either the size of the main squares or the width of the sashing strips as necessary to give a good fit on the top of the bed. The sides and bottom of the quilt include borders approximately ⅝in (1.5cm) wide on both sides of the animal print fabrics and these, too, can be made wider or narrower to suit the height of your bed (see page 45).

MATERIALS
- Assortment of animal print fabrics
- Brown fabric for sashing and binding, 8 × 20in (20 × 50cm)
- Fine, sew-in interfacing, 8 × 12in (20 × 30cm)
- Lightweight wadding, 10in (25cm) square
- Backing fabric, 10in (25cm) square
- Matching thread

Finished size: 7½ × 7⅛in
(19 × 19.5 cm)

2 Next, prepare the foundation fabric, which in this case is fine, sew-in interfacing. As this is a simple quilt to make, it is probably easier to draw the foundations with a ruler and sharp pencil rather than using a computer. You will need two side sections, one bottom section, and five top sections.

3 The quilt takes 28 squares of animal-print fabric, so choose which parts of your fabric to use as the main (top) squares – I chose animal heads from a Noah's Ark fabric, then added various skin patterns from other fabrics. Cut out squares ½in (12mm) larger than the finished size, to allow for sewing the blocks together. It is a good idea to cut more squares than you will need, as you are likely to discard some when you are arranging them in a pleasing design.

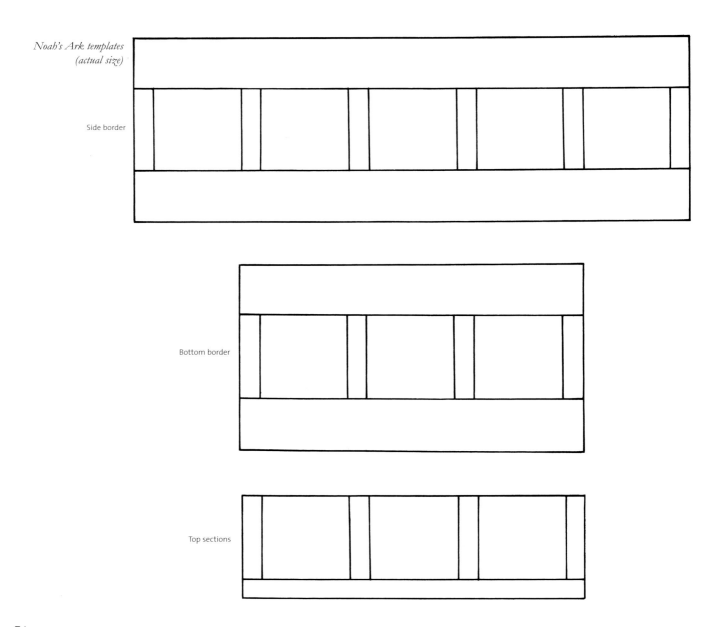

Noah's Ark templates
(actual size)

Side border

Bottom border

Top sections

HINT

To help you to choose the most interesting parts of the fabric, cut a piece of cardboard 1½in (3.8cm) square. In the centre of this, cut a square hole the same size as the blocks on the quilt, i.e. ⅞in (2.2cm) square. Move this window over the printed fabric until you see an interesting image. Draw around the outside of the cardboard template, then cut the fabric along the line you have drawn.

4 Cut five sashing strips from the brown fabric, each ½in wide × 6in long (12mm × 15cm) and cut each of these into five equal pieces. These will be used between the animal print fabrics. Cut another six strips, each ½in wide × 4in long (12mm × 10cm).

Animal print fabrics and cardboard template

5 Next, arrange the fabrics in a pleasing manner. This may take longer than you expect. I found it helpful to spread a large piece of the brown fabric on a table, and to arrange the squares on top of that.

6 I chose to use the animal heads only on the top of the quilt, and to use animal-print fabrics for the side and bottom sections. Eight of the animal prints came from fabric with a cream background and these were arranged carefully to give a balanced top to the quilt. If you look closely, you will see that most of the animals are facing left, while just the kangaroo and the lion face right. Squares with too much blue or green were discarded, and the strongest patterns, such as the zebra and tiger stripes, were put as far apart as possible.

7 Now to the sewing. Following the instructions given for foundation piecing on page 25, make up the five strips for the quilt top. Each strip starts with a small piece of the brown fabric, then an animal print square. When you have sewn pieces 1 to 7 onto the foundation, add the long sashing strip at the bottom (piece 8). Remember to trim your seam allowances to ⅛in (3mm) and press each seam well.

8 Next, join the quilt top together, being careful to match the seams to give a neat grid. Add the final sashing strip to the top, so that all the squares of animal prints are surrounded by brown fabric.

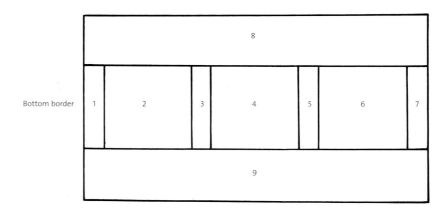

Noah's Ark fabric piecing sequence

Side border

Bottom border

Top sections

HINT

The colour of the fabric used for the sashing can make a big difference to the overall effect. I experimented with three different sashing fabrics, and also sewed the animal-print fabrics together without sashing. From these samples I decided to use a brown fabric, to give the feel of the wooden ark. However, I rejected the brown plank-effect fabric used in the test, as I felt a plainer sashing fabric would look better and also be easier to work with.

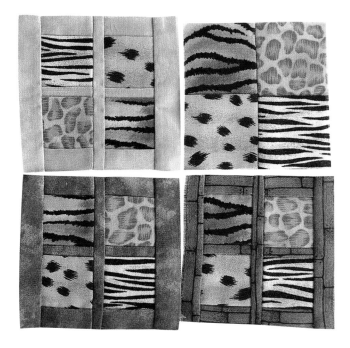

Samples of animal print fabric

9 The next step is to piece the side and bottom sections, following the same approach as you used for the quilt top. You need to check that the quilt will hang nearly to the floor when finished, so adjust the width of the borders (pieces 12 and 13) as necessary. Now you can sew the side and bottom sections to the quilt top, taking care to align the squares.

10 Follow the instructions on pages 48–57 for quilting and binding. For this quilt, I chose a lightweight cotton wadding, which has a soft feel. As it is a simple quilt, I have quilted around each square and left the borders plain. I chose to do machine quilting, but hand quilting would be equally effective.

11 The final step is to sew the binding around the outside of the quilt. I chose to use the same brown fabric that was used for the sashing and borders, so that the animal-print fabrics would really stand out. If you wish, you can sew fine wire into the top binding, as described on page 57, which will help the quilt to keep its shape on the bed.

HINT

If the quilt will be part of a permanent display, you can sew the bottom corners loosely together behind the legs of the bed. The quilt will then sit neatly on the bed.

TRIP AROUND THE WORLD

This is a traditional design, with squares arranged in a diamond pattern around a central square. For the quilt shown here, I used fabrics in lilacs and pale greens, which give a spring-like feel to the quilt.

1 First measure your dolls' house bed and adjust the pattern to fit (see page 14 for instructions). My quilt was made to fit a child's bed, so it is smaller than most other dolls' house quilts. I made each block ⅜in (9mm) square but you could, if you prefer, either increase the size of the blocks or make the quilt more than 13 squares in each direction. However, it is important that the number of rows is the same as the number of blocks across each row, and that you have an odd number. So 11 by 11 is fine, so is 13 by 13 or 15 by 15.

MATERIALS
- Assortment of lilac and green fabrics, including some floral and leaf prints
- Green fabric for binding, 6 × 4in (15 × 10cm)
- Fine, sew-in interfacing, 8 × 12in (20 × 30cm)
- Lightweight wadding, 8in (20cm) square
- Matching thread

Finished size: 5¼in (13cm) square

2 I have found that it is easier to sew neat squares which are all the same size using foundation piecing but, if you prefer, you could cut accurate squares and sew the squares together (see template below). Prepare the 13 strips of the foundation pattern on the sew-in interfacing. Refer to the chapter on using a computer to produce foundation fabric (see page 59), or draw the shapes using a ruler and sharp pencil.

Trip Around the World template (actual size)

Fabric piecing sequence

1	2	3	4	5	6	7	8	9	10	11	12	13

3 The pale green fabrics I used in this quilt were sold as a pack, and formed the starting point for my fabric selection. I added three delicate floral prints, one leaf print and various lilac fabrics. The amount of fabric needed depends where it is used in the quilt. At the very centre, only one block is needed, while some fabrics are used 20 or 24 times. Study the layout diagram to see which fabrics are used most. Cut out ¾in (2cm) squares of fabrics to allow for the seam allowances.

Trip Around the World layout

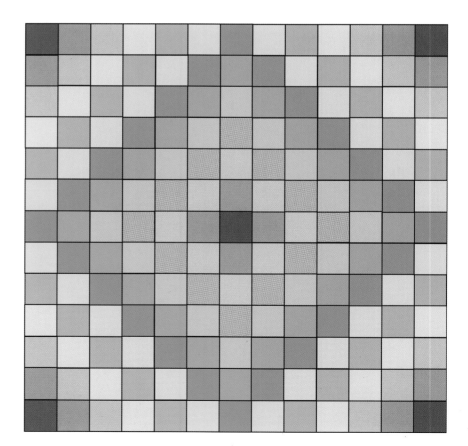

HINT
If you use a patterned fabric for the backing, any slightly irregular stitches will be less conspicuous.

4 Arrange your fabric squares on a corkboard, and pin in place. I've found that this quilt works best when there is a gradual change of colour, with only one or two dramatic changes. So, from the centre out, I have used four lilac prints, then changed to green for four blocks, then used three floral prints to change gradually back to lilac for the corners. You may need to rearrange your colour choices a few times until you are completely happy with the layout.

5 Now sew the blocks together to make 13 long strips, referring to the layout diagram to make sure you put the fabrics in the right place. It is helpful to number your strips of interfacing so that they don't become muddled (see pages 25–38 for more information on foundation piecing). Trim your seam allowances to ⅛in (3mm) and press well.

6 Next, join the strips together to make a complete quilt top. You will find this easier if you turn alternate strips around, so that the seam allowances face the other way. Pin carefully at every second corner, then sew slowly. If you enjoy hand sewing, you could sew these joining seams by hand. Press the seam allowances open, and trim to ⅛in (3mm).

7 Follow the instructions on pages 48–57 for quilting and binding. For this quilt, I chose pellon as the wadding, and sewed a small stitch at each intersection of squares. For the binding I cut 1in (2.5cm) strips and sewed these around the outside of the quilt.

HINT

Many fabric shops sell charm packs of fabric, often by colour. If you find five similar fabrics in a pack, this will make a good starting point for a colour scheme. Don't forget to vary the scale of the print – notice how some of my squares have three flowers in them, while others have only one.

DESIGN VARIATION

I have also made this simple design in bright greens and yellows, which is a more dramatic colour scheme. This time there are only eleven rows, each of eleven squares. Although all the fabrics are plains or florals, I have varied the scale of the prints to add interest and the bee fabric adds a humorous touch.

quilt 4 1000 PYRAMIDS

When I saw the bed and the matching screen below at a dolls' house show, I couldn't resist the adorable teddy bear surrounded by flowers. The challenge was then to design a quilt which would complement the bed without overpowering it. I think this little quilt is just right.

The quilt design is called 1000 Pyramids but, thankfully, there aren't quite that many in this example. I chose delicate pastel prints, with lots of different fabrics to give a scrappy effect. Since the bed has a footboard, I decided on a simple rectangle style which just drapes from side to side.

1 First measure your dolls' house bed and adjust the pattern to fit (see page 14 for instructions). The bed I used is a little shorter than many, so my finished quilt measures only 5½in (14cm) square. It is easy to make this design fit any bed, since all you need to do is add extra triangles to each strip, or to make more strips. The size of the triangles can, of course, be altered, although I wouldn't suggest making them much smaller, as you will end up with too much fabric in the seam allowances.

MATERIALS
- Assortment of pastel fabrics
- Pink fabric for binding, 7 × 4in (18 × 10cm)
- Fine, sew-in interfacing, 8 × 12in (20 × 30cm)
- Lightweight wadding, 10in (25cm) square
- Backing fabric, 10in (25cm) square
- Matching thread
- Florists' wire

Finished size: 5½in (14cm) square

2 To make your quilt the same size as mine, draw 14 rows of triangles, each with 22 complete triangles, on the interfacing. You will need seven 'A' rows and seven 'B' rows.

1000 Pyramids
templates (actual size)

Row A

Row B

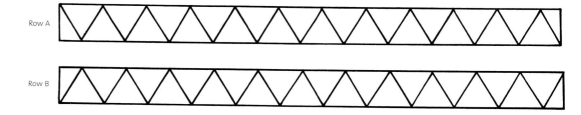

HINT

If you are using a computer to draw the foundation pieces, the best approach is to draw one triangle using the drawing tools, and change this until it is the correct size. Copy the first triangle, rotate it through 180°, and move it until it touches the original triangle. Zoom in on the image, so that it appears much larger on the screen, and check that the two triangles fit neatly together.

Once you have two triangles, join these together by grouping, then copy and paste to make two more. Join these together to make a block of four, then follow the same procedure as before, until you have the required number of triangles.

3 I used a wide assortment of fabrics in this quilt, including many tiny floral prints. The flower colours in the painted screen were my inspiration. The colours chosen are roughly equal quantities of pink, blue/violet and green/yellow. Most fabrics were used three or more times, but occasionally I only had a tiny scrap so just used the fabric once. Since this is a scrap quilt, that didn't matter at all.

4 To make sewing the pieces together a little easier, I cut out rough triangles. They were a lot larger than the finished triangles, but it is easier to start with a triangle than to use rectangles.

5 Following the instructions given for foundation piecing on pages 25–37, stitch the required number of strips. Starting at one end, lay the first two pieces of fabric that you have chosen over the first triangle. Sew the joining seam, then trim the seam allowance to around $\frac{1}{16}$inch (1.5mm) and press well. Keep adding triangles until the row is completed.

1000 Pyramids fabric
piecing sequence

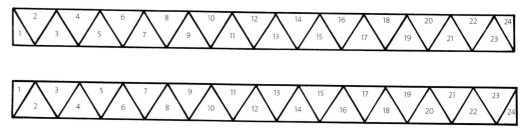

6 Although this is a scrap quilt, I tried to use the colours in even quantities, so I followed a pink triangle with a yellow or green one, then blue or violet and back to pink again. Some strips started with pink, some with yellow or green and some with blue or violet.

7 When all the strips are completed, spend some time arranging them. I turned alternate strips around so that the seam allowances would fit together better. To decide if the quilt will be balanced, you can try squinting at the quilt to see which fabrics are dominant. For instance, one particular yellow fabric stood out a little, so I kept arranging the strips until I was happy with the balance. As yellow is a dominant colour, try to use it sparingly here.

8 The hardest part of making this quilt is sewing the completed strips together. You need to be very accurate in matching the points of the triangles, so use plenty of pins. I matched the top of every second triangle, and then added extra pins to make sure the two strips stayed together. You will need to stitch slowly, and be prepared to re-do small sections of the seam if necessary.

9 Follow the instructions on pages 48–57 for quilting and binding. This quilt didn't seem to need much quilting, so I hand-stitched the layers together at each intersection of triangles. To finish, sew the binding around the outside of the quilt. I used a delicate pink fabric the same colour as the bed, and added florists' wire to the top and bottom bindings.

DESIGN VARIATION
This simple quilt design would look fantastic in blue and white, or stunning in citrus shades. Why not try a few different colour combinations?

quilt 5 BLACK AND WHITE TRIANGLES

This is a very easy quilt to make, as each block contains just three pieces. The black and white fabrics make it a dramatic quilt, which would suit a modern dolls' house.

1 First measure your dolls' house bed and adjust the pattern to fit (see page 14 for instructions). I used three different sizes of blocks – ⅞in (2.2cm) square for the central blocks, and ⅞ × 1in (2.2 × 2.5cm) for the blocks at the edges. The corner blocks are 1in (2.5cm) square. This gave me the white trellis effect in the middle of the quilt and sharp white points at the edge. You can alter the size or the number of blocks as necessary to suit your bed.

2 For a quilt the same size as mine, you will need 64 blocks in total – 36 central blocks, 4 corner blocks and 24 border blocks. Draw the designs on the interfacing using a ruler and sharp pencil, or use your computer to produce the foundation fabric.

MATERIALS
- Assortment of black and white fabric scraps, 1¼in (3cm) square
- Black fabric for borders and binding, 10 × 8in (25 × 20cm)
- White fabric for diagonal lines, 6 × 8in (15 × 20cm)
- Fine, sew-in interfacing, 16 × 12in (40 × 30cm)
- Lightweight wadding, 10in (25cm) square
- Backing fabric, 10in (25cm) square
- Matching thread

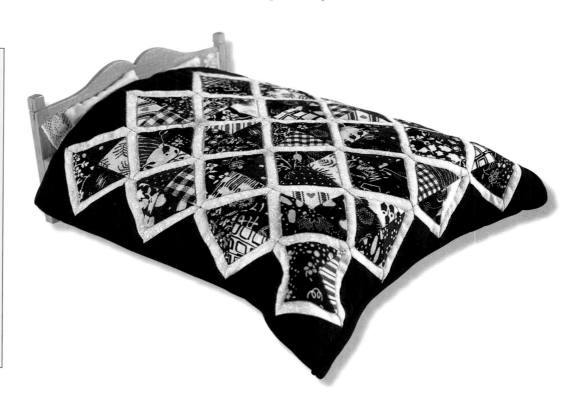

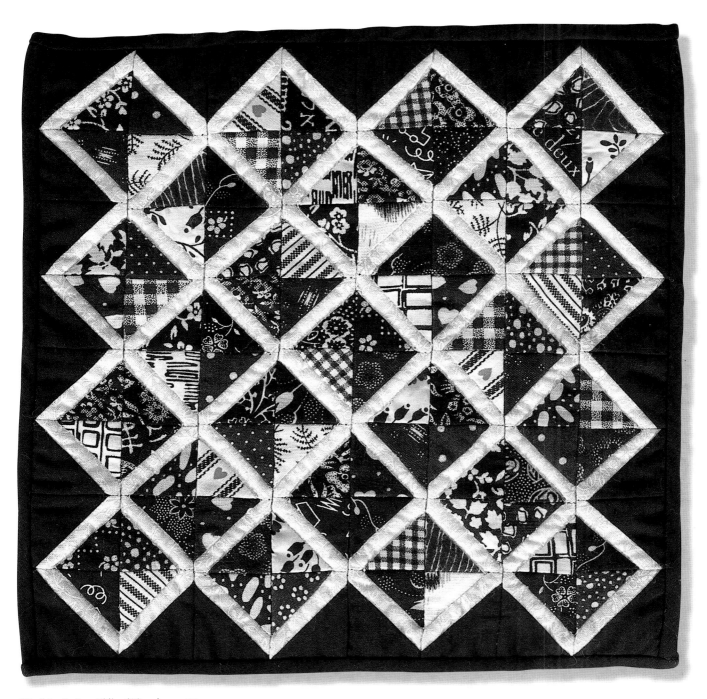

Finished size: 7½in (19cm) square

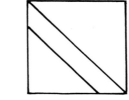

Corner blocks

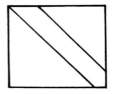

Border blocks

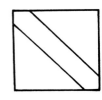

Central blocks

Black and White Triangles templates (actual size)

3 Most of the fabrics used in this quilt were scraps leftover from the full-size quilts my mother makes. Look for black and white fabrics with small prints, and make sure you include spots and stripes. Cut each 1¼in (3cm) square across the diagonal to give two triangles.

HINT

Adding a small amount of a different colour is a good idea. Notice how the three tiny red hearts are arranged to form an irregular triangle, which makes your eye move across the quilt. Any bright colour will do – you could, for instance, try lime green, periwinkle blue, or any shade of yellow.

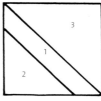

Corner blocks

Border blocks

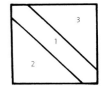

Central blocks

4 Make the 36 central blocks first. Start by cutting the white fabric into ½ × 1½in (12mm × 3.8cm) strips. Place one of these on the foundation interfacing to cover the diagonal section of the design, then sew a black and white triangle in position 2. Trim the seam allowance and press the seam. Add another triangle as piece 3, trim and press as before, and you have completed your first block.

5 Continue until all 36 central blocks are made. To create an interesting quilt top, try not to use any of the black and white prints more than four times.

6 Now for the border blocks. These are made in the same way as the central blocks, but every border block uses plain black fabric for piece 2. Notice that triangle 3 is smaller than triangle 2. The four corner blocks are made in the same way as the border blocks, with plain black fabric as piece 3.

7 Arrange your completed blocks into eight rows of eight blocks. The top and bottom rows are made from corner and border blocks, while the other six rows need a border block at each end. If you have used an accent colour, place these to form an irregular triangle.

8 Sew all the blocks together into rows, and press the seams in alternate directions. That is, press the seams up on row one, down on row two and so on. Join the rows together to form the quilt top, matching the corners of the blocks.

9 Layer the quilt top with lightweight wadding and backing fabric. I used pellon as the wadding in this quilt and a patterned white fabric for the backing. Refer to Finishing Your Quilt, pages 48–57, for guidance on quilting and binding. I machine quilted around each black and white diamond using white thread.

If you prefer hand sewing, use small stitches and stay on the white fabric, as this avoids seam allowances which are difficult to sew through.

10 Make the binding from strips of plain black fabric cut 1½in wide × 10in long (3.8 × 25cm). Sew these around the outside of the quilt, and slipstitch neatly in place on the reverse of the quilt.

HINT
Using a walking foot on your sewing machine will ensure that you have accurate lines of machine quilting.

quilt 6 RED LOG CABIN

Log Cabin is one of the earliest patchwork designs, and is easy to make using foundation piecing. I chose rich red fabrics for this little quilt to bring out the warmth of the dark wood of the scroll-end bed (shown below). Although from a distance the quilt looks like simple red and cream stripes, if you look closely you will see that there are many different fabrics used.

At the centre of each block I have used a daisy on a red background, and this was the inspiration for my colour scheme. To choose other fabrics I laid them against the daisy fabric to check the colour. This quilt is comparatively quick to make, because there are only 25 blocks altogether.

1 First measure your dolls' house bed and adjust the pattern to fit (see page 14 for instructions). The finished size of the quilt pictured is 5½in (14cm), so I used log cabin blocks measuring just over 1in (around 2.8cm). If you are making a quilt to fit a much larger bed, it would be better to make more quilt blocks, rather than increase the size of each block.

MATERIALS
- Assortment of red and neutral fabrics
- Dark red fabric for binding, 7 × 4in (18 × 10cm)
- Cream fabric for border, 7 × 3in (18 × 8cm)
- Fine, sew-in interfacing, 8 × 12in (20 × 30cm)
- Lightweight wadding, 7in (18cm) square
- Backing fabric, 7in (18cm) square
- Matching thread

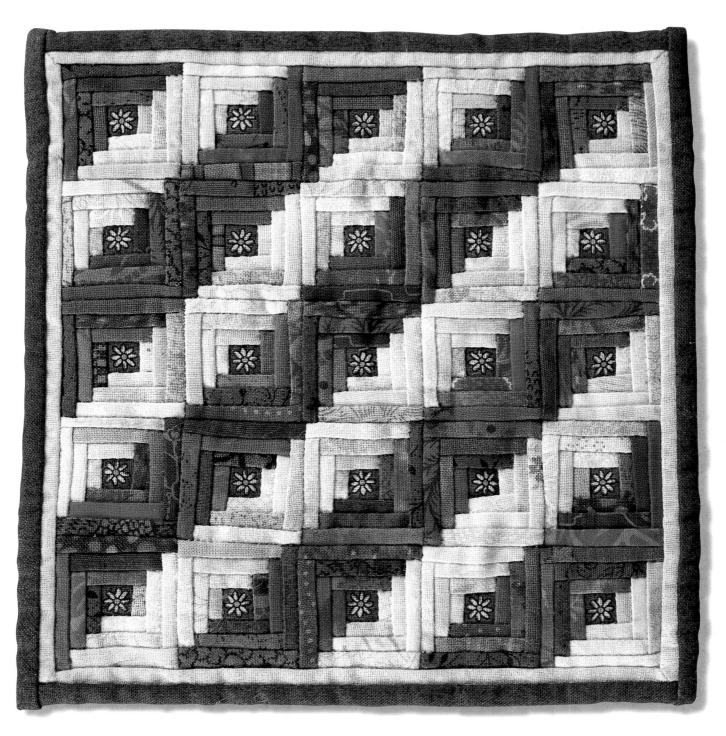

Finished size: 5½in (14cm) square

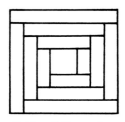

*Red Log Cabin template
(actual size)*

2 Draw 25 foundation blocks using a ruler and sharp pencil, or follow the instructions given in Using a Computer (see page 59) to produce foundation blocks.

3 Select your fabrics, bearing in mind that you can use very small scraps if you wish. In total, I used around 30 different reds and 30 different neutral fabrics in the project. The reds included some rusty orange shades and some deep burgundies, while the neutral went from pale cream through to biscuit and coffee shades. The subtle variation in colour gives depth to the quilt.

4 I cut rectangles approximately ½ × 1½in (12mm × 3.8cm), although even smaller pieces can be used near the centre of each block. Altogether you will need 150 red strips and 150 neutral strips. You can cut all the pieces before you begin sewing, or as you go along, if you prefer.

> **HINT**
>
> **Store the fabric rectangles in small zip-lock bags and label the outside. It is also helpful to put completed blocks in a separate bag. It is surprisingly easy to lose miniature patchwork and advisable to warn loved ones not to throw out even tiny pieces of fabric without checking.**

5 Sew the 25 blocks, following the instructions given in the Foundation Piecing chapter (see pages 25–38). With log cabin, you start with the centre square then build up gradually all around. If you have chosen a motif for the central square, you will need to position this carefully as you start.

> **HINT**
>
> **To position a motif in the central square, hold the fabric and the interfacing up to the light and move the interfacing until you can see a motif framed by the central square. If you have a light box, this is an easy task. Otherwise, use a window on a sunny day, or a work lamp.**

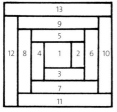

*Red Log Cabin fabric
piecing sequence*

6 Starting with neutral fabrics, sew strip 2 in place. The quickest way to make this quilt is to position the central square and sew strip 2 in place on all 25 blocks at the same time, then snip the blocks apart and press the seams. You can, of course, make each block separately, or make them in batches of five if you prefer, but I would recommend sewing all the blocks at the same time, since, for best results, you will want to change thread colours as you move from neutral to red fabrics and vice versa.

7 The first two strips (pieces 2 and 3) are neutrals, then you sew two red strips in place (pieces 4 and 5). Remember to press carefully as you sew, and to trim the seam allowance so that it doesn't get caught up in the next seam. In this quilt, that will mean

a seam allowance of less than ⅛in (3mm). While that may seem far too narrow if you are used to full-sized patchwork, remember that these quilts will not usually be washed or handled in the same way as full-sized quilts.

8 Keep sewing the strips around the central motif until the blocks are completed. I tried to make sure that I used a range of fabrics in each block, so that the dark reds, orangey reds and different neutral shades were spread across the quilt.

9 When all the blocks are complete, arrange them into a pleasing design. If you have used only 25 blocks, you are limited in the possible arrangements. However, if your quilt is 6 × 6 blocks, or 8 × 8 blocks, you can produce a zigzag effect, or have diamonds radiating from the centre. Some possible log cabin layouts are shown below.

10 Follow the instructions in the Finishing Your Quilt chapter (pages 48–57) for quilting and binding. For this quilt, I chose lightweight polyester wadding, and used the red and cream daisy fabric for the backing. I quilted along the diagonal lines by hand, using red thread to match the backing fabric and tried to make sure that the tiny stitches were hidden in the seams.

11 To finish, sew a narrow cream border around the quilt, using strips of fabric ¾in (2cm) wide. I used a dark red fabric cut into 1in (2.5cm) strips for the binding. Since the quilt was to be tucked under the mattress of the scroll-end bed, it didn't need florists' wire in the binding (but see page 57, if you wish to insert some).

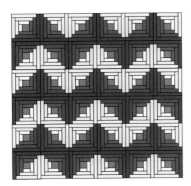
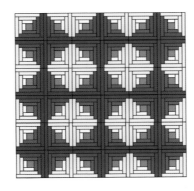
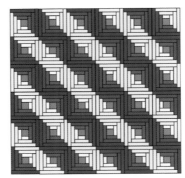

Log Cabin layouts

quilt 7 APPLIQUE HEARTS

This lovely quilt uses a different approach from foundation-pieced patchwork, and would be perfect in a lady's bedroom. Using silk for the background and backing makes a lightweight quilt which drapes beautifully over the bed.

1 As I made this quilt to fit a bed with corner posts, I decided on a quilted top with plain sides and bottom. You will need to measure your dolls' house bed and adjust the pattern to fit (see Getting Started, page 14, for instructions). You can either alter the number of hearts you use, or just place them closer together or further apart.

MATERIALS
- Assortment of red and pink fabrics, each 1in (2.5cm) square
- Cream silk, 10 × 20in (25 × 50cm)
- Lightweight wadding, 10in (25cm) square
- Iron-on adhesive (e.g. Bondaweb/Vliesofix), 4 × 5in (10 × 13cm)
- Matching thread for machine sewing
- Silk thread for hand quilting

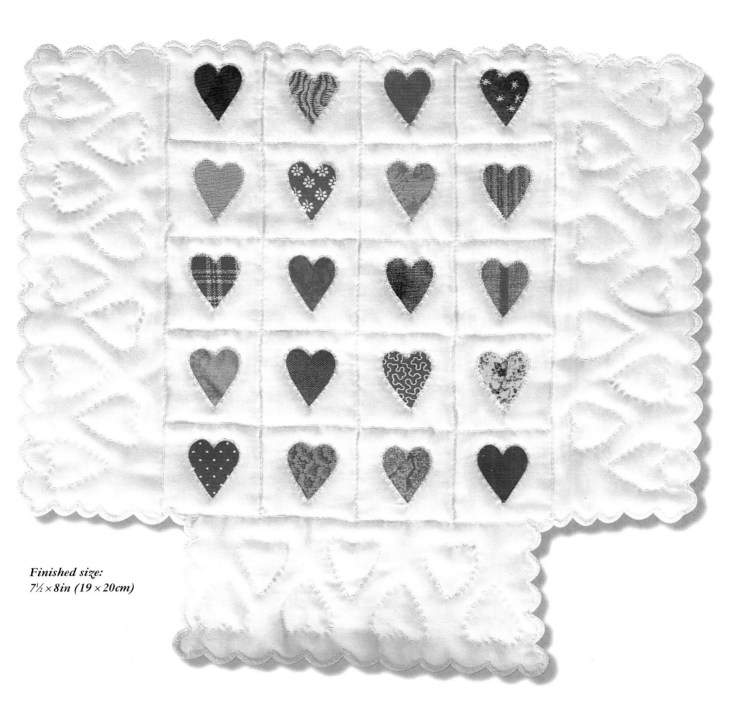

Finished size:
7½ × 8in (19 × 20cm)

95

The heart motif
template (actual size)

2 The cream silk I used came from a scarf, but you could use an old blouse or new fabric bought especially for this project. Cut a rectangle the length of your finished quilt and twice as wide, plus 1in (2.5cm) all round. Fold this in half, and press carefully – this should give you two layers of silk approximately 10in (25cm) square.

3 Next choose the fabrics for the hearts – since they are so small, you can use scraps of fabric. Cut the iron-on adhesive into 20 small pieces roughly 1in (2.5cm) square, and iron each one on the back of a fabric scrap, making sure that the backing paper is in place.

HINT

If you wish to draw your own heart motif, there is an easy way to make the design symmetrical: fold a piece of paper in half, and draw half a heart next to the fold. Cut it out round the unfolded side, open the paper, and you have a perfect heart.

4 Trace the heart motif from this page, and cut out. Draw round this onto the paper backing of the iron-on adhesive, and cut the hearts out carefully. Peel off the paper backing so that the hearts will stick to the silk background when ironed.

5 The next step is to place the hearts carefully in position and iron them on, using a warm iron (i.e. on a silk setting). Since the silk I used was fine and slightly transparent, I was able to mark the position of the hearts on graph paper, and place this between the two layers of silk. In this quilt the hearts are 1⅛in (3cm) apart, so you need to draw 20 dots on graph paper at the correct intervals. Place the bottom point of each heart on a dot, make sure it is straight, and iron carefully, then remove the paper guide from between the layers of silk.

6 Place the wadding between the two layers of silk, and pin around the outside to form a silk and wadding sandwich. I used silk wadding because it drapes beautifully over a bed, but also has plenty of 'loft', so the hand quilting shows up well. Sew carefully between the hearts to set each one inside a square, either by hand or machine.

7 I usually recommend quilting before finishing the edges of a quilt. However, for this quilt I found it better to quilt as the final step. If your sewing machine has a pretty scalloped edge stitch, as mine does, you could use this to finish the edges. You will need to sew a stitch sample using scraps of silk and wadding to check that the length and width of the scallop looks right in 1/12 scale. When you are happy with the effect, sew carefully around the edges. Trim the silk and wadding close to the stitching, being careful not to snip the threads by mistake. If you prefer, you can add a binding as explained in Finishing Your Quilt, pages 54–7, instead of sewing a scalloped edge.

HINT

You can mark the edges of the quilt with masking tape before sewing the scalloped edging, to keep your lines straight. If you do this, be sure to remove the tape within four hours, otherwise it may mark the quilt top.

8 Finally, quilt around each heart and fill the plain silk border with quilted heart motifs. I used cream silk thread for quilting, to match the lustre of the background fabric. Use a fine needle and the smallest stitches that you can manage, and make sure that you are working in good light, either daylight or a work lamp.

9 For the borders, trace the heart shape onto paper a few times, and cut out carefully. Use small pieces of double-sided sticky tape to hold the hearts temporarily in position on the quilt. Move the shapes around until you are happy with the pattern, then quilt around with tiny stitches. Alternatively, cut heart motifs from freezer paper and iron in place. Remove after quilting.

DESIGN VARIATION

Why not try this quilt with a different motif, such as butterflies or flowers? Or a yellow quilt with tiny teddy bears would make a lovely cot quilt.

quilt 8 SQUARE WITHIN A SQUARE

This is a simple little quilt to make, based around a fabric with a repeating pattern of lilies on a greenish-blue background. When I saw it, I thought it would make a lovely quilt with alternate blocks of flowers and patchwork.

1 I made the quilt for the elegant provincial-style bed, 4¾in wide × 6in long (12 × 15cm), shown below. I decided to have five blocks across the top of the bed and six down, so the finished size of each block needed to be a little under 1in (2.5cm). However, as blocks often 'shrink' a little when they are sewn together and then quilted, I worked with 1in (2.5cm) blocks. Adding patchwork blocks across both the sides and the bottom of the quilt resulted in a quilt seven blocks by seven. You may need to alter the size of the blocks slightly to fit your bed – if so, see instructions on page 14.

MATERIALS
- **Floral fabric: approx. 12in (30cm), or sufficient to cut 25 identical motifs**
- **Assortment of blue and pink fabrics, each 3in (8cm) square**
- **Blue fabric for border and binding, 10in (25 cm) square**
- **Fine, sew-in interfacing 16 × 12in (40 × 30cm)**
- **Lightweight wadding, 10in (25cm) square**
- **Backing fabric, 10in (25cm) square**
- **Matching thread**
- **Florists' wire**

Finished size: 7½in (19cm) square

2 Draw the foundation patterns on the fine, sew-in interfacing. See Using a Computer, page 59, for instructions, or draw the shapes using a ruler and sharp pencil. You will need 24 patchwork blocks, and 25 empty squares.

Square Within a Square templates (actual size)

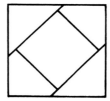 

> **HINT**
>
> **I have used identical motifs in each floral block, to give a formal effect, but the quilt would also be effective with random floral blocks. You may find a few floral fabrics in similar colourways that you could use together.**

3 Consider the colours of your main fabric and decide which to emphasize in the patchwork blocks. I chose eight greenish-blue fabrics and eight different pinks for the patchwork blocks and used each fabric three times.

4 Following the instructions given in the Foundation Piecing chapter (see pages 25–38), sew 24 patchwork blocks. Since each block is made of only five pieces, they are quick to make. Start with a 1in (2.5cm) square of pink fabric in the centre. Cut 1in (2.5cm) squares of blue fabric, then cut these across the diagonal to give two triangles. I chose to mix up the fabrics so that no two blocks are exactly the same.

Square Within a Square fabric piecing sequence

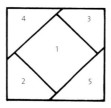 

5 Sew the empty squares onto the back of the floral fabric, centring your motif. This may seem like an unnecessary extra step, but I have found that it is much easier to ensure that the blocks are square if you do this. If you prefer, you can draw squares directly on the back of the fabric instead.

> **HINT**
>
> **To select a suitable floral fabric, cut a 1in (2.5cm) square 'window' out of a small piece of cardboard. Move this window across a floral fabric until you see a motif that you like (see facing page). It is a good idea to carry a little card window in your purse, so that you can 'audition' suitable fabrics whenever you see them.**

6 Next, play about with the arrangement of the patchwork blocks until you are happy with the layout. I found it easier to leave the floral blocks on one side, and focus on the square-within-a-square blocks. Remember to step back from your layout and check that any brighter fabrics are distributed evenly across the quilt. Add in the floral blocks to give a chequerboard effect, then pin all the blocks to a corkboard until you are ready to sew them together.

7 Sew the blocks together into seven rows, making sure that the floral blocks all face the same way, then press all the seams towards the floral blocks. Join the seven rows together, matching the corners of the blocks.

Lilies fabric with cardboard window

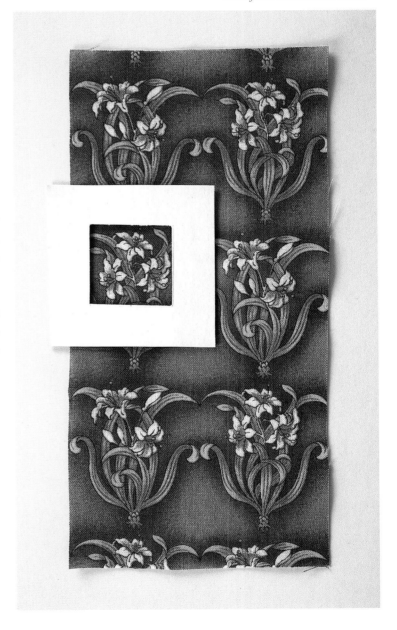

8 For the border I cut strips of greenish-blue fabric ¾in (2cm) wide and sewed these carefully around the outside of the quilt. When the binding was sewn in place, only ¼in (6mm) of the border strips remained visible.

9 Follow the instructions in Finishing Your Quilt, pages 48–57, for quilting and binding. For this quilt, I chose a thin layer of silk wadding, and cotton lawn for the backing. I used machine quilting, and sewed close to each of the diamonds in the patchwork blocks. If you choose to quilt by hand, try to keep your stitches an even size and close to the diamonds. You will need to use stab stitching when you cross over seam allowances.

10 Finally, sew the binding around the outside of the quilt. Inserting florists' wire in the top and bottom bindings helps the quilt to stay neatly on the bed (see instructions for this on page 57).

quilt 9 TROPICAL FISH

I made this quilt as part of a Noah's Ark bedroom I prepared for display at a dolls' house exhibition in 2001 (see picture on page 104). The first quilt I made for the roombox was the Noah's Ark quilt on page 73 but, having painted the lower half of the bedroom walls sea blue, I decided I needed lots of fish swimming on the bed!

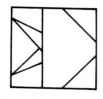

Tropical Fish template
(actual size)

1 First measure your dolls' house bed and adjust the pattern to fit (see page 14 for instructions). As I designed this quilt to fit a single bed with footposts, I made each fish block ⅞in (2.2cm) square. You could alter the size of the fish or just change the size of the sashing strips between them.

2 For this quilt you will need 28 fish blocks. Use a ruler and sharp pencil to draw the design on the interfacing, or refer to the Using a Computer chapter (pages 59–65), for instructions on producing foundation fabric.

MATERIALS
- **Assortment of bright fabrics, each 2in (5cm) square**
- **Greenish-blue fabric for background, 8 × 20in (20 × 50cm)**
- **Fine, sew-in interfacing, 8 × 12in (20 × 30cm)**
- **Lightweight wadding, 10in (25cm) square**
- **Backing fabric, 10in (25cm) square**
- **Matching thread**
- **Florists' wire**

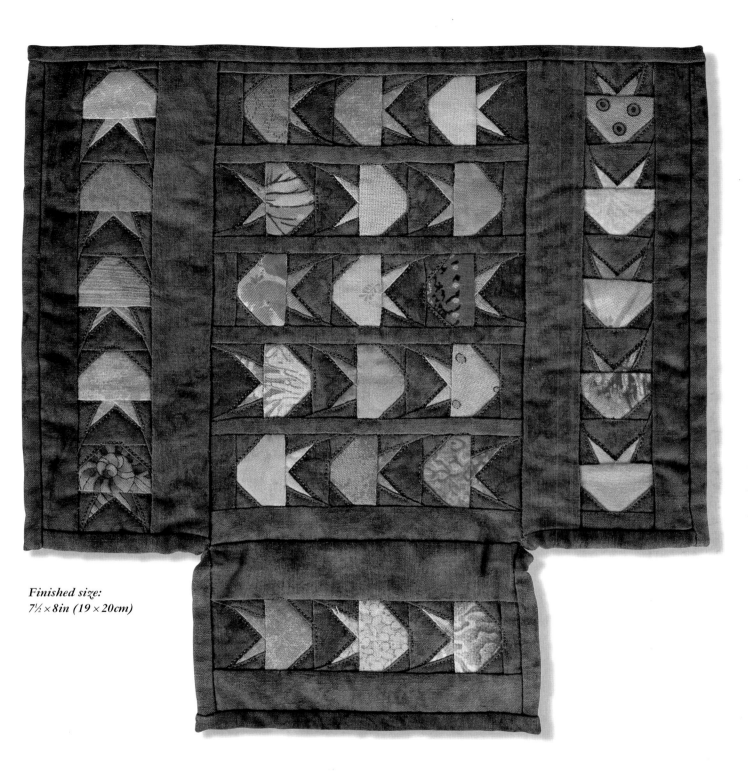

Finished size:
7½ × 8in (19 × 20cm)

103

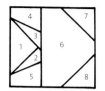

Fish block fabric-piecing sequence

3 Start with your main fabric, and choose bright colours which show up well against it. Since this quilt was designed for a little girl's bedroom, I chose pink, yellow and orange as my fish colours, but it would look equally effective in shades of turquoise, green and yellow. Every fish is made from a different fabric in my example, but you could use each fabric two or three times.

Noah's Ark roombox with Tropical Fish quilt

4 See pages 31–4 for detailed instructions on making this fish block using foundation piecing. Following this step-by-step approach, make all 28 fish blocks.

5 Arrange the patchwork blocks to give a balanced quilt top. You will need 15 fish for the top of the quilt, 5 for each side and 3 for the bottom. I chose to have the rows of fish swimming in alternate directions on the top of the quilt.

6 Join the blocks together into rows, with ¼in wide (6mm) sashing strips in between the fish, then join the rows for the quilt top together, again with ¼in (6mm) sashing strips to separate the fish.

7 Decide how long you wish the quilt to be, and determine the width of the border strips. The finished size of my strips was ⅝in (15mm). Sew the fish blocks together for the sides and bottom, and add the border strips. Sew the sides and bottom of the quilt onto the top.

8 Refer to Finishing Your Quilt, pages 48–57, for guidance on quilting and binding. For this quilt, I chose pellon for the wadding, and machine quilted close to the outline of each fish. I used the same greenish-blue fabric for the binding around the outside of the quilt, so that the brightly coloured fish would show up well.

I really enjoyed decorating this roombox and making small items like mobiles to hang from the ceiling. I'm sure I will add more items over the years.

HINT

If you don't have the time or money for a complete dolls' house at this stage, you could make a roombox to display one of your quilts. Roomboxes are usually made from MDF with a perspex front to protect the contents from dust and they can, of course, be any size you wish.

quilt 10 AMISH-STYLE ROMAN STRIPES

This is an easy design to make using foundation piecing, and particularly effective in these colours, which are inspired by Amish quilts. Most Amish people live in America, and they choose to live a simple life. They don't drive cars or use electricity, and they wear practical clothes in plain colours. Their quilts are also designed to be practical, and often feature black or dark grey as the main colour. Serving God and helping others in their community is very important to Amish people.

My first attempt at making this quilt used grey cotton as the main fabric, but that proved to be too stiff, so for the one shown here I used grey silk from a second-hand blouse. Using silk for more than half of the quilt produces a softer effect which drapes well over a miniature bed.

MATERIALS
- Assortment of plain fabrics in bright colours (see stage 3), each 2in (5cm) square
- Grey silk for main fabric, 8 × 18in (20 × 45cm)
- Binding fabric, 8 × 6in (20 × 15cm)
- Fine, sew-in interfacing 8 × 12in (20 × 30cm)
- Lightweight wadding, 8in (20cm) square
- Backing fabric, 8in (20cm) square
- Matching thread

Finished size: 6¼in (16cm) square

1 First measure your dolls' house bed and adjust the pattern to fit (see page 14 for instructions). You can alter the size of the central blocks if you need to, or make the borders a different width. I used blocks ⅞in (2.2cm) square.

2 Prepare 25 foundation blocks using fine, sew-in interfacing. For instructions on producing foundation fabric, refer to the chapter on Using a Computer, pages 59–65, or draw the shapes using a ruler and sharp pencil. If you prefer, you can draw five rows each of five blocks, which makes it easier to join the blocks together later.

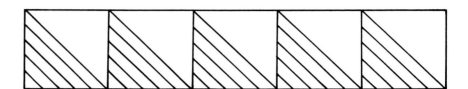

Roman Stripes template (actual size)
Row of five blocks template

3 Next, select some plain fabrics – I used 25 different shades of blue, pink and purple, ranging from very pale to deep, intense colours to go with my grey silk main fabric. Cut each 2in (5cm) square of fabric into five narrow strips, so that you have 125 strips of fabric for the Roman stripes.

HINT

If your fabric collection does not include any plain fabrics, look carefully at the background of large prints. You may be able to cut plain strips from between the motifs. Also, check the wrong side of your dark fabrics: many dark tone-on-tone prints have a plain reverse.

4 Following the instructions given for foundation piecing, make up your 25 blocks. Please note that you will need to start with a triangle of grey fabric and then add strips of colour. This is essential if you have decided to make five strips of five blocks, and makes the quilting process easier. Try to ensure that the different and dominant colours are spread throughout the quilt, and that you use fabrics in different positions in the blocks. For example, if you look closely at my quilt you will see that the white fabric appears in positions 2, 3, 4, 5 and 6, so some strips are long and some are short.

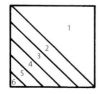
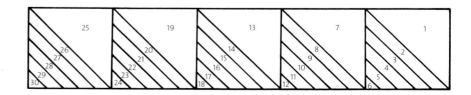

Roman stripes fabric-piecing sequence
Row of five blocks

5 Arrange your blocks, then sew them together to make five rows of five blocks. Join the rows together.

6 Amish quilts often have wide borders, with detailed hand quilting in them, so cut strips of your grey backing fabric 1½in (3.8cm) wide and sew these to the top and bottom of the quilt, and then to the sides. Amish quilts do not have mitred borders, as this uses more fabric and is considered wasteful.

7 It is impossible to recreate the beautiful hand-quilting designs of Amish quilts in 1/12 scale. However, if you can, add hand quilting rather than machine quilting. I used silk wadding, then quilted with dark grey thread across the diagonal of each block.

8 For the borders, I chose a simple, curve design and used grey thread a little lighter than the main fabric. I cut the quilting template out of freezer paper and ironed it lightly onto the front of the quilt. After I had sewn around it, I removed the template, then quilted a second line of stitches ¼in (6mm) inside the first line. Further information on quilting and binding is given in Finishing Your Quilt, pages 48–57.

HINT
This design also looks lovely in different colours. You do, however, need strong contrasts between the fabrics. The baby's play mat pictured below is far less effective than the Amish-style quilt, partly because the fabrics blend too much into each other, and partly because the fabrics always appear in the same positions.

Quilting template

9 Finally, sew the binding around the outside of the quilt. I chose a bright colour for the binding, in keeping with many examples of Amish quilts, and used bias strips.

Roman Stripes play mat

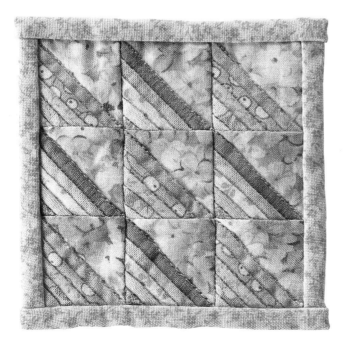

quilt 11 RIOTOUS PENNANTS

This was the first miniature quilt I made using foundation piecing. Although it is not as accurate as many of the later quilts in this book, it remains one of my favourites. It was inspired by the 'Pennants' quilts in Kaffe Fassett's book *Patchwork* (see Bibliography, page 178), and ended up much brighter than I intended – hence 'riotous pennants'.

1 This little quilt fits on a bed with no footboard or posts. It can, of course, be altered to fit other beds (see Getting Started, page 14, for instructions). The main part of the quilt is approximately 5 × 6in (12.5 × 15cm), with the two borders adding 1½in (3.8cm) to the sides and bottom.

2 There are three parts to this quilt – the central blocks, each 1in (2.5cm) square and the two borders (see templates on page 112). Prepare 30 central blocks, of which 15 should be Block A and 15 should be Block B. Draw these onto fine, sew-in interfacing using a ruler and sharp pencil, or refer to the chapter on Using a Computer, pages 59–65, for instructions on producing foundations. You also need bottom and side borders, both narrow and wide. The diagrams are shown actual size.

MATERIALS
- Assortment of blue, green, yellow and orange fabrics, each 6in (15cm) square
- Orange fabric for binding, 6 × 10in (15 × 25cm)
- Fine, sew-in interfacing, 16 × 12in (40 × 30cm)
- Lightweight wadding, 10in (25cm) square
- Backing fabric, 10in (25cm) square
- Matching thread

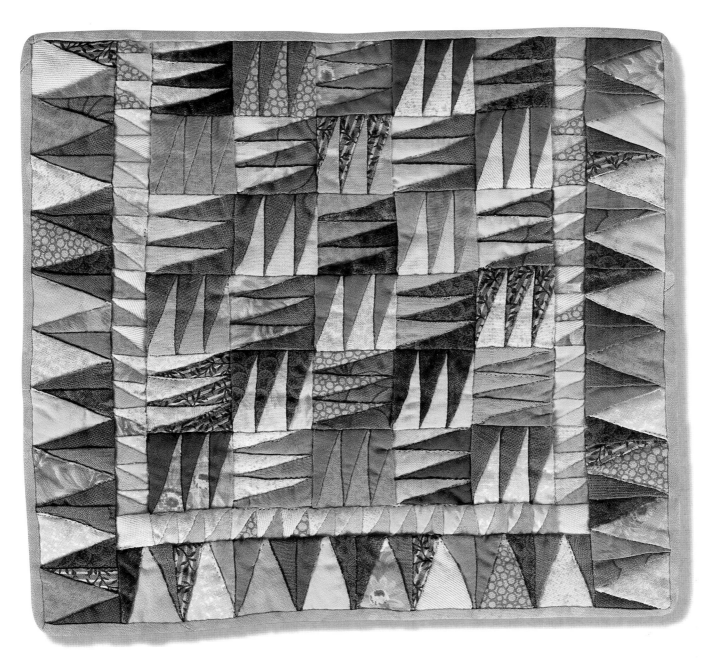

Finished size: 8 × 7½in (20 × 19cm)

Templates

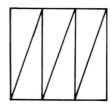

Central Block A

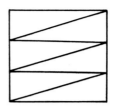

Central Block B

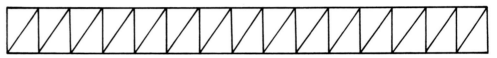

Narrow bottom border

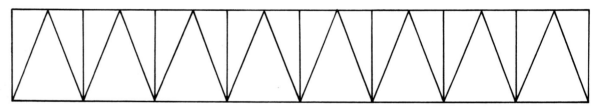

Wide bottom border

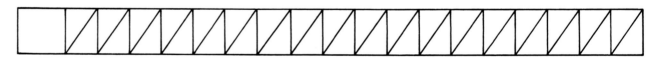

Narrow side border

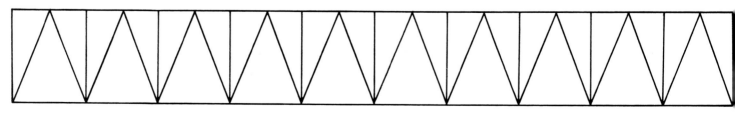

Wide side border

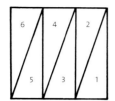

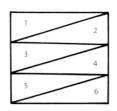

Fabric-piecing sequence

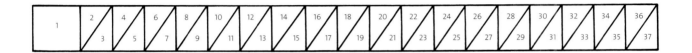

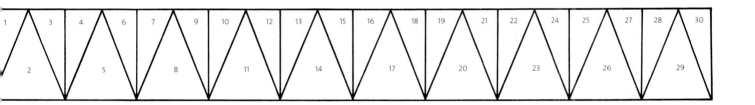

3 To produce a quilt similar in feel to the one I made, shown on page 111, choose strong, bright colours, and use four different fabrics in each of the colours. The narrow border uses only yellow and orange fabrics, while all the colours appear again in the wide border.

HINT

Remember to take regular breaks from your sewing. It is hard to concentrate for more than one hour on 1/12 scale patchwork, and you are likely to start making mistakes if you become tired. Try a few stretching exercises, and make sure you focus your eyes on distant objects for a few minutes to prevent headaches.

HINT

The narrow border is the most fiddly part of the quilt to make. If you prefer, you could attach a plain narrow border in yellow, rather than the small triangle blocks.

4 Following the instructions given for foundation piecing on pages 25–38, make up the 15 A blocks and the 15 B blocks in the following colour combinations:

Block A	green/yellow	3	Block B	green/yellow	4
	green/orange	4		green/orange	4
	blue/yellow	4		blue/yellow	3
	blue/orange	4		blue/orange	4

Please note that you should always start the foundation piecing with either yellow or orange fabric: these colours are used for pieces 1, 3 and 5 in each block. For my quilt, I worked with rectangles of fabric, cut to roughly 1½×½in (38 ×12mm). Each block is made up of just two fabrics.

Layout of A and B blocks

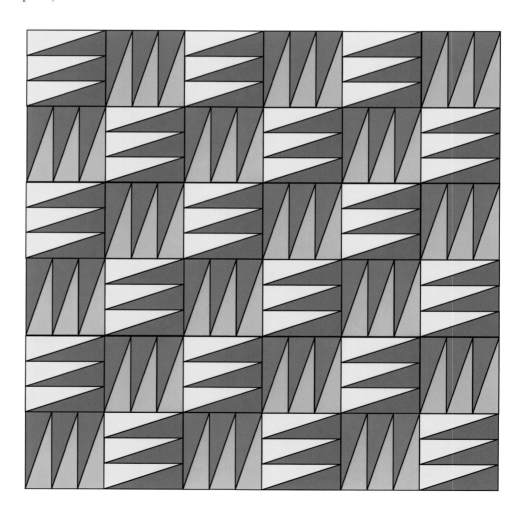

5 When all the central blocks are made, arrange them to form the quilt top. Arrange blocks A and B in a chequerboard pattern, with the blue or green fabric always at the left in A blocks and at the bottom in B blocks. Sew the blocks together to make six rows of five blocks, and press the joining seams towards the A blocks. Join the rows together, taking care to match the seams.

6 Make up the narrow border using orange and yellow fabrics. Sew these onto the quilt top, with the orange fabrics at the outside of the border.

7 Prepare the wide borders, using yellow/orange fabrics for the large triangles and green/blue fabrics for the divided triangles. Sew the wide bottom border onto the quilt, then add the side borders. Press the quilt top well, and trim any loose threads.

8 The next step is quilting. Choose a lightweight wadding and backing fabric, each approximately 10in (25cm) square. Following the instructions in the Finishing Your Quilt chapter, pages 48–53, add lines of machine or hand quilting to emphasize the blocks. I used transparent thread and machine quilted only the B blocks in the centre and the large triangles in the wide border.

9 Finish the quilt by binding the edges (see instructions on pages 55–7). I used ¾in (2cm) bias strips cut from hand-dyed orange fabric.

quilt 12 HEARTS

I used a lovely soft pink fabric for the background of this quilt, with hearts in many shades of pink and red. The heart block is not difficult to piece, and you can easily adjust the size of the finished quilt by altering the width of the sashing strips between the hearts.

1 First measure your dolls' house bed and adjust the pattern to fit (see Getting Started, pages 14–17, for instructions). You can alter the number of heart blocks you make, or use wider sashing strips between the blocks. I made my hearts just over ¾in (2cm) square and used ⅕in (5mm) sashing strips.

2 Prepare 49 heart blocks from the foundation fabric – I used fine, sew-in interfacing. Refer to the chapter on Using a Computer (pages 59–65) to produce foundation fabric, or draw the shapes using a ruler and sharp pencil.

MATERIALS

- Assortment of pink fabrics, each 3in (7.5cm) square
- Pink fabric for background and binding (e.g. cotton lawn), 10 × 20in (25 × 50cm)
- Dark pink fabric for borders, 8 × 3in (20 × 7.5cm)
- Lightweight wadding (e.g. silk), 10in (25cm) square
- Backing fabric, 10in (25cm) square
- Matching thread
- Florists' wire

Finished size: 7¼ × 8in (19.5 × 20cm)

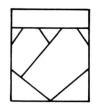

Heart template (actual size)

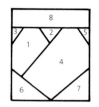

Heart fabric-piecing sequence

My block arrangement

3 Choose your main fabric first, then select other fabrics which show up well against it. I chose 12 different pink and red fabrics, and used them four times each. The central pink fabric appears only once. You can, of course, use more than 13 fabrics if you have suitable colours. For the Ruby Hearts wallhanging, pictured on page 120, I used different fabrics for most of the 40 hearts.

4 Make up the 49 heart blocks following the instructions given in the Foundation Piecing chapter, page 25. I found it easiest to cut two rectangles of heart fabric approximately the correct size, and then cut small and large triangles from the background fabric. It is important to remember to press well each time you sew on another piece of fabric.

5 Spend some time arranging the hearts, until you are happy with the balance of colours. If you have used each fabric (except the central one) four times, you may wish to follow my arrangement of blocks.

6 Next join the hearts together into seven strips of seven. Press the seams towards the pink rectangles which separate the blocks. Cut ten strips of the pink background fabric 8 × ¾in (20.5 × 2cm), and attach seven of these to the left side of each strip of hearts. Join the strips together, being careful to make the sashing strips an even width and as straight as possible.

7 Add the three remaining strips to the top, bottom and right of the quilt top. Press the quilt well, as it will not be possible to press the seams after quilting.

8 Follow the instructions for quilting and binding (see pages 48–57). For this quilt, I chose cotton lawn for the backing fabric and used silk wadding. Carefully machine quilt around each heart, keeping your stitches small and very close to the outline of the heart. I found that finishing off the ends of the quilting thread took much longer than the actual quilting, but it is essential to ensure the quilting does not unravel.

9 The final step is to sew the binding around the outside of the quilt. First, sew a border of dark pink fabric to frame the heart blocks, using ¾in strips (2cm). Then use the main pink fabric for the binding. Because I wanted to tuck the bottom of the quilt under the mattress, I sewed florists' wire into the top and bottom hems to help me do this (see instruction for this on page 57).

While I was writing this book, my parents celebrated their fortieth wedding anniversary. I wanted to make a wallhanging for them, and decided to alter the design of the little hearts quilt I had made. I made the heart block twice as big and put an even larger heart in the centre. I called the wallhanging 'Ruby Hearts' because ruby is the stone used to commemorate 40 years of marriage, and hearts, of course, symbolize love.

For the main fabric I used a silk shirt bought at a charity shop, while the hearts are made from various fabrics, including cotton, silk and velvet. I had great fun with my children choosing all shades of orange, red and purple – passionate colours! I arranged the fabrics to flow from orange in the top left corner to darkest purple in the bottom right. As I often do, I spent most of one evening trying out different fabrics, until I was happy with the arrangement.

These 40 fabrics were used to make the heart blocks, which were then joined together in rows, with the large central heart taking the place of nine smaller hearts. If you look very closely, you will see my parents' names and wedding date in the log cabin strips under the central heart.

If you wish to make this Ruby Hearts wallhanging, which is shown overleaf, you can follow the instructions given above for the Hearts quilt, using the larger template shown on page 121. I added a few beads for decoration once the quilting was completed.

HINT
When you are making such small quilts, it is hard to quilt accurately by machine without a walking foot. If you plan to make a number of dolls' house quilts, it is a great investment to buy one for your machine.

Ruby Hearts wallhanging
14 x 14¼in (35.5 x 36cm)

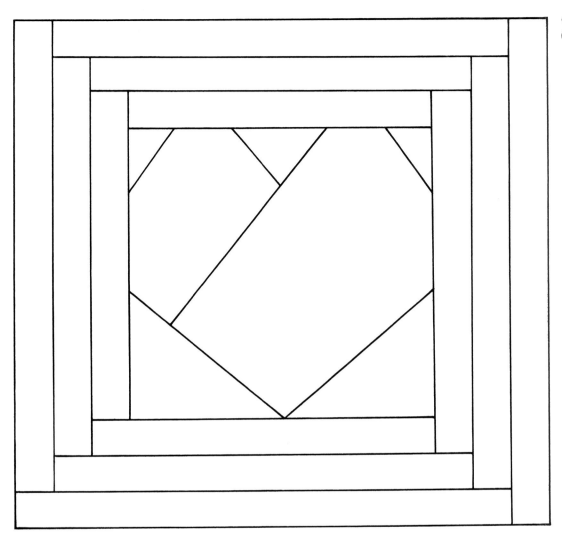

*Central heart template
(actual size)*

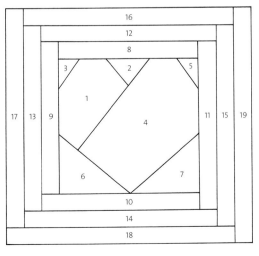

*Central heart
fabric-piecing
sequence*

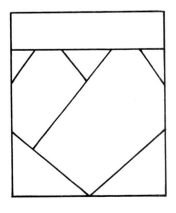

*Large hearts template
(actual size)*

quilt 13 BLUE WINDMILLS

Although this quilt looks complex, it is surprisingly easy to make. The blue silk I used for the background fabric resulted in a soft quilt which drapes well over the bed, and the blue and white fabrics look crisp and fresh: a classic combination for a quilt.

1 The quilt was made to fit a simple wooden bed, 4½in wide by 6¼in long (11.5 × 16cm). I made a quilt top of 1in (2.5cm) blocks, then added borders for the sides and bottom and this helps the quilt to sit well on the bed. Measure your dolls' house bed and adjust the pattern to fit (see page 14 for instructions). You could make the blocks a little smaller if you need to, and the borders are easy to alter.

2 Each block is made from two pieces, so you need to draw 60 foundation patterns on the interfacing. Refer to Using a Computer (page 59) to produce foundation fabric, or draw the shapes using a ruler and sharp pencil. You will also need three border sections. My border rectangles are ¼ × ½in (6 × 12mm), which is the same size as the rectangles in the quilt top.

MATERIALS
- **Assortment of blue and white fabrics, each 2in (5cm) square**
- **Lightweight blue silk for background and binding, 12 × 20in (30 × 50cm)**
- **Fine, sew-in interfacing, 16 × 12in (40 × 30cm)**
- **Lightweight wadding (e.g. pellon), 10in (25cm) square**
- **Backing fabric, 10in (25cm) square**
- **Matching thread**

Finished size: 8in (20cm) square

Blue Windmills template, central block, (actual size)

Border template (actual size)

3 For the background, I chose blue silk, which was left over from a blouse I had made. You could use new silk, or buy a second-hand garment from a charity shop or, if you prefer, you could use lightweight cotton instead of silk.

4 Lay your background fabric out on a table, and place other blue fabrics against it. I chose pale blue prints as well as blue and white fabrics. You will need pieces 1 × 2in (2.5 × 5cm) for the central blocks and about the same amount of each print for the borders. If you choose to use 30 different fabrics, as I did, you will only need a 2in (5cm) square of each one. If you prefer, you could use fewer fabrics, but you will then require more of each.

5 For each block, you will need four rectangles of the blue silk and four rectangles of a patterned fabric. The finished size of the rectangles is ¼ × ½in (6 × 12mm), so start with rectangles approximately ½ × ¾in (12 × 18mm). Following the instructions given in the Foundation Piecing chapter, page 25, place a rectangle of patterned fabric on the interfacing to cover section 1, put blue silk on top of it, then sew the seam joining piece 1 to piece 2. Trim the seam and press open carefully. Piece 3 is patterned fabric, then use blue silk for piece 4 and you have made half of a block.

6 Make the other half of the block exactly the same. Join the two half-blocks together, matching the central seam and doing your best to keep the rectangles straight. Trim the central seam to ⅛in (3mm) and press open. You should see a little windmill appear in the centre of the finished block.

7 Sew the other 29 blocks in the same way – I recommend sewing a few at a time, so that you don't have to move constantly from the sewing machine to the ironing board. When all 30 blocks are complete, arrange them into five rows of six blocks. Sew the blocks into rows, then join the rows together, matching the corners of the blocks. Press the joining seams open, then press the quilt top well.

HINT
If you have friends who make full-sized quilts, why not see if you can have their fabric scraps? Many quilters throw away pieces as large as 1 x 2in (2.5 x 5cm) which are perfect for miniature quilts.

Windmill fabric-piecing sequence

	1	2
	3	
	4	

Windmill fabric-piecing sequence

Border layout

| 1 | 2 | 3 | 4 | 5 | 6 | 7 | 8 | 9 | 10 | 11 | 12 | 13 | 14 | 15 | 16 | 17 | 18 | 19 | 20 | 21 | 22 | 23 | 24 | 25 | 26 | 27 | 28 | 29 | 30 |

31

8 Next, make the borders. I made this quilt to fit a low bed, but you could make your borders wider if your bed is higher than mine. Start by sewing the rectangles of patterned fabric onto the interfacing, trimming the seams and pressing well as you go. I needed 29 rectangles on each side border and 30 across the bottom – you can do more or less to suit the size of your bed.

9 Cut three strips of blue silk, 8 × 1½in (20 × 3.8cm). Sew these onto the border interfacing, then attach the borders to the quilt top. (See page 45 for more information on borders.) I decided to mitre the corners of the borders but, if you wish, you can sew the bottom border on first then add the side borders.

10 Next, press the quilt top and borders well, as you cannot press after quilting. I used pellon for my wadding and more of the blue silk for the backing fabric. Quilt either by hand or machine. I used the walking foot on my sewing machine and quilted a cross in each of the plain blue windmills, which made the patterned windmills stand out even more.

11 Finish the quilt with a narrow binding around the outside.

HINT
Plain-coloured fabrics show every quilting stitch, so it is better to use a patterned backing until you are confident with your quilting.

quilt 14 FLYING GEESE

This is a traditional design which is much easier to make than it looks. Here, the purple colour scheme gives a restful, feminine feel, and accentuates the purple beads on the lovely brass bed, while the gold fabrics echo the brass.

1 It is easy to adjust this quilt to any size of bed, since you can alter the width of the plain purple sashing strips or change the number of 'geese' in each strip. Measure your dolls' house bed and decide how many strips of geese to make, and how wide the sashing strips should be (see page 42 for guidelines).

2 Draw the design onto the fine, sew-in interfacing. To produce foundation fabric, refer to the chapter on Using a Computer (page 59), or draw the shapes using a ruler and sharp pencil. To make the quilt exactly as shown here, you will need seven foundation strips, each with 22 geese triangles, plus one bottom strip of 16 geese.

(see page 42 for guidelines). ... (page 59)

MATERIALS
- Assortment of pink and purple fabrics, plus a small amount of gold fabric
- 8in (20cm) length, or a fat quarter, of purple fabric for background, sashing strips and binding
- Fine, sew-in interfacing, 8 × 12in (20 × 30cm)
- Lightweight wadding, 10in (25cm) square
- Backing fabric, 10in (25cm) square
- Matching thread
- Florists' wire

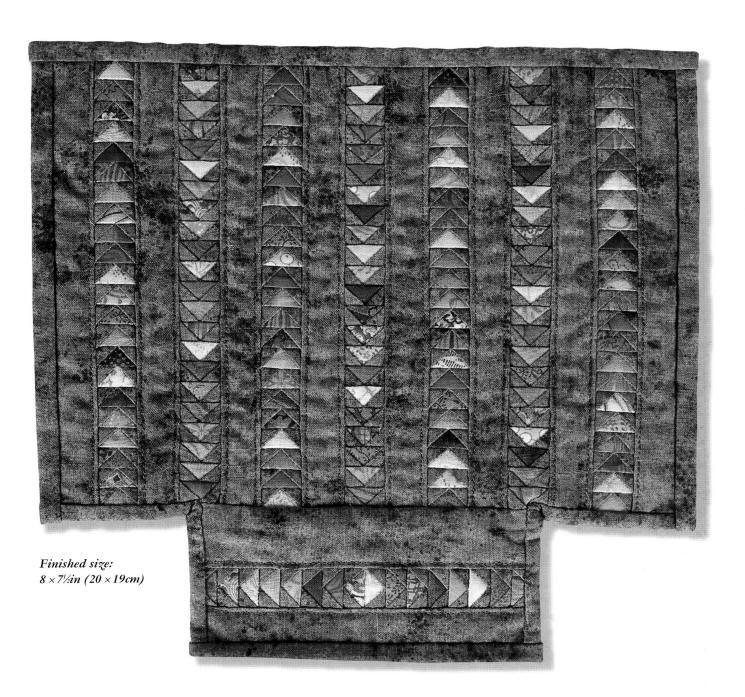

Finished size:
8 × 7½in (20 × 19cm)

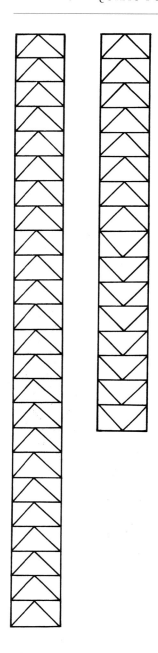

Flying geese (actual size)

3 I started with the soft purple main fabric, and chose pinks and purples to go with it. Some of my pieces of fabric were only one 1in (2.5cm) square, which was enough to make two 'geese'. I used around 40 different fabrics, but the quilt would also look effective with fewer fabrics. To brighten the quilt I found a purple and gold fabric, and a plain gold, both of which I have used sparingly.

4 Following the instructions given in the Foundation Piecing chapter, pages 25–38, make up the strips of geese: cut rectangles approximately 1 × ½in (2.5 × 1.25cm) for the geese, and for the purple triangles, cut ¾in (2cm) squares and then cut these in half across the diagonal. You could cut all the fabrics before you begin sewing, but I prefer to cut pieces as I go, as such small bits of fabric are easily lost.

5 Start with a pink or purple rectangle as piece 1, then sew purple triangles in place to be pieces 2 and 3. Trim the seams, press well, then add another rectangle in a different colour. Continue until you have sewn all 22 'geese' in place. Make the other six long strips in the same way. Try to ensure that the different pinks and purples are spread evenly through the quilt.

6 When you have finished the strips of geese, you need to join them together. I chose to have some geese flying up the quilt while others fly down, but all the geese flying in the same direction would also look good. Cut strips of the main fabric 7 × 1in (18 × 2.5cm) and sew these to the left of each row of geese. Sew all the strips together carefully, trying to make the geese line up across the quilt. Add a final strip of the main fabric on the right hand side, then press these long seams towards the purple sashing strips.

7 To suit the style of the brass bed, I also needed a strip of geese across the bottom of the quilt. I made this in the same way as the long strips, except that the geese fly in two directions, out from the middle. Sew the bottom strip of geese in place, using a sashing strip of the purple fabric.

8 Finish the project by quilting and binding as you wish (see instructions in Finishing Your Quilt, pages 48–57). I used silk wadding for this quilt, and machine quilted straight lines on each side of the strips of geese. I used the same purple fabric for the binding, and decided not to use florists' wire as the quilt sits well without it.

DESIGN VARIATION

The flying geese design would also look lovely with a cream background, and lots of bright colours.

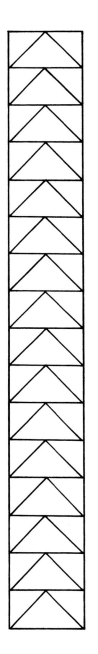

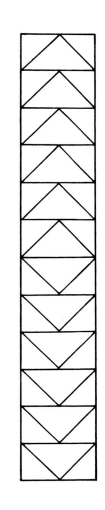

Larger template (actual size)

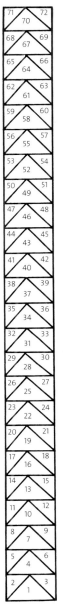

Flying geese fabric-piecing sequence

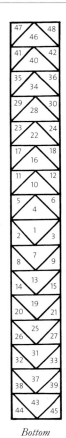

Bottom border

quilt 15 SUNSET LOG CABIN

This quilt was inspired by a beautiful winter sunset over southern Sydney in Australia, where I live. The sky was darkening gradually from clear blue and the clouds were streaked with delicate yellows and oranges. I selected fabric colours that evening and made a sample block. Thankfully there was a similar sunset a few days later which allowed me to check and alter my original fabric choices.

1 First measure your dolls' house bed and adjust the pattern to fit (see Getting Started, page 14, for instructions). I made this quilt for a simple bed without a footboard or footposts, and worked with 1in (2.5cm) blocks. If your bed is smaller than mine, I suggest making fewer blocks rather than changing the size. You could miss out four blocks from each lower corner if you have footposts on your bed.

2 For this quilt you will need 64 foundation blocks, all the same. I used fine, sew-in interfacing for the foundations, and printed them from my computer. Refer to Using a Computer (page 59) for instructions on producing foundation fabric, or draw the shapes using a ruler and sharp pencil. Note that this is not a regular log cabin block with all of the strips the same size. Instead, the blue pieces are wider than the yellow/orange, giving a slight curve to the design.

MATERIALS
- **Assortment of yellow, orange and blue fabrics**
- **Pale blue sky-patterned fabric, 10in (25cm) square**
- **Orange fabric for binding, 10 × 6in (25 × 15cm)**
- **Fine, sew-in interfacing, 16 × 12in (40 × 30cm)**
- **Lightweight wadding, 10in (25cm) square**
- **Backing fabric, 10in (25cm) square**
- **Matching thread**
- **Florists' wire**

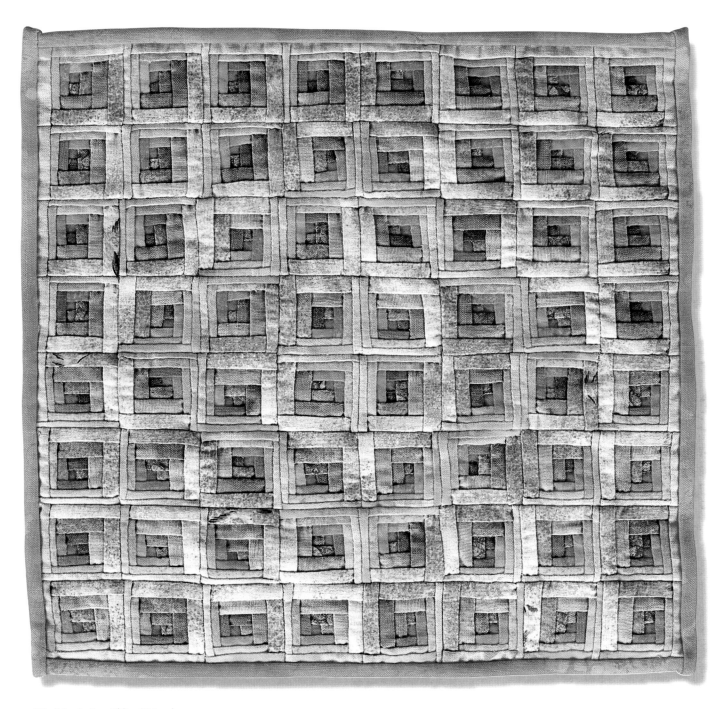

Finished size: 7¼in (20cm) square

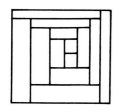

Sunset Log Cabin template (actual size)

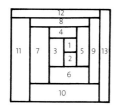

Sunset Log Cabin fabric-piecing sequence

3 I used pale yellow, mid-yellow, orange, pale blue and mid-blue fabrics. As a minimum, you will need two of each of the different colours plus the sky-patterned fabric and a deep orange for the centre of the blocks. Consult the log cabin diagram below, showing the fabric-piecing sequence, for the position of each colour. I chose to use 18 different fabrics for this quilt so that the blocks are not all identical. The centre of each block has dark orange and mid-blue fabrics, while the outside has pale yellow and a lovely sky-patterned fabric which is pale blue and white.

4 To sew log-cabin blocks, start with the centre square and work outwards. (See the Foundation Piecing chapter, page 26, for a detailed example of log cabin patchwork.) On the yellow/orange side of each block, cut the seam allowances very close to the stitching, to avoid them getting caught in the next seam you sew.

HINT

I recommend making a sample block before you make all 64 foundation blocks. My first attempt at this quilt mostly used the same fabrics as the finished quilt, but I put the pale prints in the centre and the dark fabrics at the outside. The result was much too heavy and too orange. I added the sky fabric and a paler yellow fabric, then reversed the position of the pale and dark fabrics in the block and I am very pleased with the delicate, airy effect this gave to this quilt.

Sample log cabin block

> **HINT**
> If you are unsure whether to use hand or machine quilting, consider whether you have large pieces of fabric or small pieces with lots of seams. It is difficult to do machine quilting when there are lots of seams, so use invisible hand quilting instead.

5 Remember to use the darker colours at the centre of each block and the pale ones at the outside. On the blue side of the block, the last two strips are both cut from the sky-patterned fabric and, if you look hard at the quilt, you will see a few seagulls in the sky.

6 Arrange the log cabin blocks, and pin them to a corkboard until you are ready to sew them together. There are many different ways to arrange log cabin blocks which can give zigzags across the quilt or lines radiating from the centre. The layout you choose is entirely up to you – look at the quilts in the Gallery (pages 160–77) for more ideas, or the Red Log Cabin quilt on page 91.

7 Follow the instructions in the Finishing Your Quilt chapter for quilting and binding (pages 48–57). For this quilt, I chose pellon as the wadding and used tiny hand-quilting stitches. If you decide to do hand quilting, try to lose the stitches in the seams between the blue and yellow fabrics.

8 Finally, sew the binding around the outside of the quilt. Cut strips of orange fabric 1½in (3.5cm) wide and attach the binding to the sides first, then to the top and bottom. I sewed florists' wire into the top and bottom bindings to help shape the quilt on the bed.

quilt 16 PEACH NINEPATCH

Ninepatch is a traditional patchwork design, so-called because there are nine small squares within the completed block. Many books of quilt designs contain ninepatch blocks, and they may help you to choose colours for your quilt. Here, I have used various peach fabrics and alternated the ninepatch blocks with plain squares – the overall effect is calm, and I can easily imagine this quilt in a dolls' house bedroom.

1 First measure your dolls' house bed and adjust the pattern to fit (see Getting Started, page 14, for instructions). As I designed this quilt for a bed with a footboard, I needed 48 × 1in (2.5cm) squares. For your bed, you may need to make more or fewer blocks, or alter the size of each block slightly.

2 I made 24 ninepatch blocks, and alternated these with 24 plain squares of fabric. This not only meant that the quilt was quicker to make, it also made joining the blocks together much easier. Bear in mind that, if all the blocks are ninepatches, there are lots of seams to match, while using plain blocks makes this process more straightforward.

MATERIALS
- **Assortment of peach fabrics, 3in (7.5cm) square**
- **Fabric for binding, 10 × 6in (25 × 15cm)**
- **Fine, sew-in interfacing, 16 × 12in (40 × 30cm)**
- **Lightweight wadding, 8 × 10in (20 × 25cm)**
- **Backing fabric, 8 × 10in (20 × 25cm)**
- **Matching thread**

Finished size: 6 × 8in (15 × 20cm)

Ninepatch template (actual size)

3 Each ninepatch block is made in three parts which are then sewn together to make the complete block. For 24 blocks you will therefore need 72 small foundations. Refer to Using a Computer (page 59) to produce foundation fabric, or draw the shapes using a ruler and sharp pencil.

4 I started by choosing 24 different peach fabrics for my plain squares. These fabrics were also used in the ninepatch blocks. I then added a few floral prints to my selection, which also introduced a little green into the colour scheme. Each ninepatch block uses two different prints, so you need a range of pale and darker peach fabrics. You may not have as many fabrics to choose from as I did but this quilt would be equally effective with less variation between the blocks.

> **HINT**
>
> **Note that the ninepatch design uses two fabrics placed in a chequerboard pattern. It is important to make sure that two of your little strips have dark fabric at the outside with a pale central block, while the other has a dark central block and pale outside sections.**

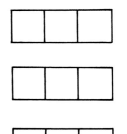

Ninepatch blocks

5 Make up the ninepatch blocks, following the instructions in the Foundation Piecing chapter (see page 25). Press each little strip carefully. When you sew the small strips together, turn the middle strip around so that the seam allowances fit together snugly. Press the seam allowances open with your fingers, then press firmly with an iron.

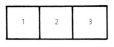

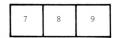

Ninepatch fabric-piecing sequence

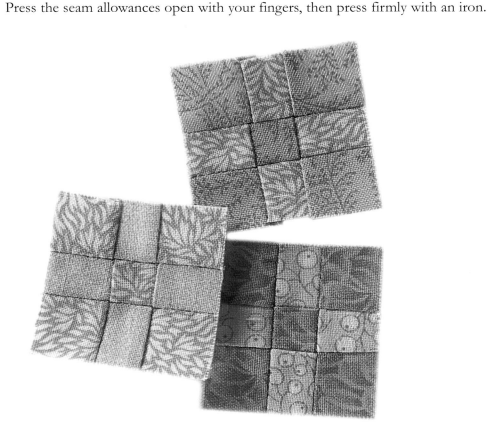

HINT

If some of your prints are peach and white, and seem too bright, try dyeing them with tea to soften the effect. In a small bowl, make a weak solution of tea, and place a small piece of fabric in it for a moment. Rinse immediately to remove excess tea. If the fabric is still too pale, soak for a little longer, or try a stronger solution of tea. Fabrics take on colour differently, so dye one fabric at a time.

The colour from tea dyeing may fade in time, so you may prefer to use a commercially available fabric dye which gives the same soft colour.

6 To ensure that the plain peach squares were exactly the same size as the ninepatch blocks, I printed out 24 blocks from the computer onto interfacing, each 1in (2.5cm) square. I sewed these to the reverse side of the peach fabrics, then cut out the squares. If you prefer, you can draw squares on the back of the fabric.

7 Arrange your ninepatch blocks on a corkboard, making sure that the darker colours are spread throughout the quilt. Add in the plain fabric squares. When you are happy with the arrangement, pin the blocks to the board to keep them in the correct order.

8 Join the blocks into rows of six to run down the bed, and press the seam allowances away from the ninepatch blocks. Join your rows together, matching the corners as neatly as you can.

9 Follow the instructions on pages 48–57 for quilting and binding. For this quilt, I used silk wadding, and hand quilted with running stitches between the blocks. For the binding I cut 1in (2.5cm) bias strips from one of the peach fabrics. Since I had decided to tuck this quilt under the mattress of the bed, I did not need to sew florists' wire into the binding.

The effect of tea dyeing

quilt 17 LIGHTHOUSE AND BOATS

When my son was two-and-a-half-years old, my mother made him a wonderful quilt, with lots of different boats around a lighthouse. This project, a very simplified version of Benjamin's quilt, would look lovely in a child's room in your dolls' house.

Although each boat is made from three pieces which are later joined, the quilt is quite straightforward to make. I have made it in two different colourways to show how choosing different fabrics can alter the look of the finished quilt.

1 I made this quilt to fit this simple wooden bed, with a headboard and footboard. If you need to alter the size, I suggest changing the width of the borders.

MATERIALS
- Assortment of blue and red fabrics, plus small pieces of brown and gold
- Dark blue fabric for sashing and binding, 10 × 12in (25 × 30cm)
- Fine, sew-in interfacing, 8 × 12in (20 × 30cm)
- Lightweight wadding 8in (20cm) square
- Backing fabric, 8in (20cm) square
- Matching thread
- Embroidery cotton in brown, yellow and gold

Finished size: 6½ × 6¼in (16.5 × 16cm)

*Lighthouse and Boats
templates (actual size)*

*Lighthouse and Boats
fabric-piecing sequence*

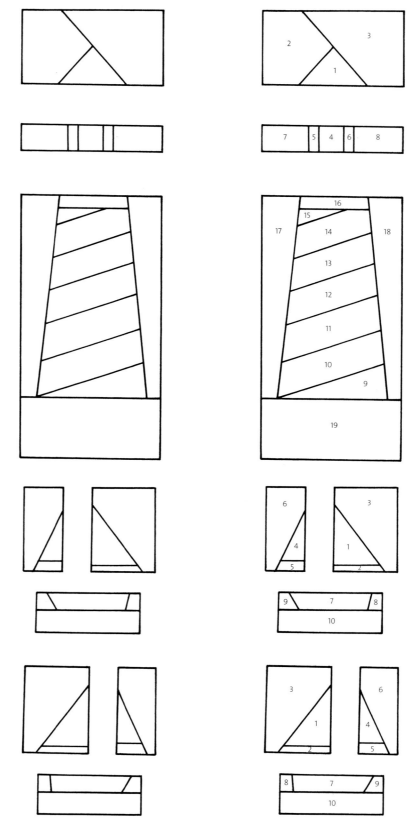

2 Draw the foundation patterns on the interfacing using a ruler and sharp pencil. You will need one lighthouse and six boats in total, with three facing left and three facing right. I suggest you prepare the borders later, after the boats have been made.

3 I decided to make each of the boat blocks different, so I needed six sky fabrics, six sea fabrics and six boat fabrics. For the sails, I used a scrap of cream silk. The lighthouse block uses a seventh sky fabric, as well as a scrap of metallic gold fabric for the light and I searched out a mottled brown fabric which resembles rock for the lighthouse to stand on.

4 Following the instructions given in the Foundation Piecing chapter (see pages 25–38), make up the sail and sky sections. Join them together, and press the central seam open. Make up the boat sections, and join these to the sails, then press the seam towards the boat.

5 Embroider a mast on each boat with brown embroidery cotton, and add a little flag at the top of the mast if you wish. Join the boats to make two strips, each with three boats. Again, press the seams towards the boat section.

6 Using foundation piecing, make up the three sections of the lighthouse. The pattern has diagonal lines so that you can make a striped lighthouse. However, if you prefer, you can use a striped fabric as I did in the second boats quilt.

7 If you want to frame the lighthouse and boats with a very dark blue fabric, as I did, cut six strips, each 5in long by ¾in wide (12 × 2cm). Join a strip of dark blue to each side of the boats, then sew the lighthouse section in between. The finished width of the blue strips should be ¼inch (6mm). Finally, sew the remaining two strips top and bottom and the centre of the quilt is complete.

Border template
(actual size)

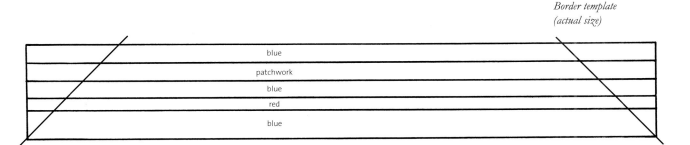

| blue |
| patchwork |
| blue |
| red |
| blue |

HINT

It is hard to make accurate mitred corners in 1/12 scale, so you may prefer to make a more simple border. See some different suggestions for borders on pages 45–8.

8 Next, make up the borders. I chose to make striped borders with mitred corners, which frame the patchwork blocks like a picture. Measure the centre of the quilt, and check the size: mine measured 4¾ × 4½in (12 × 11.5cm). Draw the striped border onto interfacing, altering the size if necessary and making sure that the lines at the corners are drawn at 45°. You will need two shorter borders for the sides and two longer borders for the top and bottom.

9 Use small pieces of blue fabric varying in width from ⅜–¾in (1–2cm) for the patchwork stripe in the middle of the border. Add plain blue strips on either side, then a narrow strip of bright red. Finish with another dark blue stripe. Attach the borders to the boats and lighthouse. Because you will be sewing the mitred seams, it is important to stop sewing a few stitches before the corner of the central block.

10 To sew the mitred seams at the corners, fold the quilt in half across the diagonal, and pin one corner seam. Open the quilt out, and check that the stripes match up, and that the quilt lies flat. Sew the seam carefully, then pin and sew the other three corners. See page 47 for more information on mitred borders.

11 Layer the quilt top with the wadding and backing fabric. I used pellon for the wadding as it is very light. I decided to do a minimal amount of machine quilting, and merely outlined the rectangles containing the lighthouse and the boats.

12 Finally, sew the binding around the outside of the quilt. I used the dark blue fabric again, so that the boats, lighthouse and red border really stand out.

DESIGN VARIATION

For the second colourway shown on the facing page I chose a greeny-blue fabric as the main colour, and used soft green instead of bright red. This time all the boats are identical, and the lighthouse was made with a striped fabric. The result is a quieter quilt because there is less contrast between the colours. I added hanging loops and a dowel rod to make this into a little picture.

quilt 18 STARS

The bright stars seem to leap off the black background of this quilt and, although it is a complicated quilt to make, it is worth the effort. If you are able to use a computer to prepare the foundation blocks, it will help you to achieve a more accurate result.

1 Measure your dolls' house bed and adjust the pattern to fit (see Getting Started, page 14, for instructions). I made the quilt to fit this single bed, and fitted each star inside a ⅞in (2.3cm) square. You could make the star blocks a little larger, or use wider strips at the sides if your bed is taller.

2 Draw the foundation patterns on to the interfacing using a ruler and sharp pencil, taking care to make the lines accurate. As mentioned above, use a computer to prepare the foundation blocks, if possible, as this quilt is complex and requires good foundations (see Using a Computer, page 59, for instructions). Each star is made in two halves, so you will need a total of 66 half-star blocks for a single bed quilt.

MATERIALS
- **Assortment of bright fabrics, each 2in (5cm) square**
- **Black fabric for background and binding, 8 × 40in (20 × 100cm)**
- **Fine, sew-in interfacing, 16 × 12in (40 × 30cm)**
- **Lightweight wadding, 10in (25cm) square**
- **Backing fabric, 10in (25cm) square**
- **Matching thread**
- **Florists' wire**

Finished size:
6⅜ × 7⅞in (16 × 20cm)

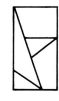

Star templates (actual size)

3 For a single bed quilt you will need 33 different bright colours, while for a double bed you will need 47 fabrics. I decided to use eight groups of colours – yellow, orange, red, pink, lilac, blue, turquoise and green – with four fabrics from each colour group. I added an extra green fabric as my thirty-third choice. You could, of course, use fewer fabrics and make three or four stars from each fabric, rather than making all the stars different.

I started with more than 33 fabrics, and tried each one out against the black background, narrowing the choice until I was happy with the selection.

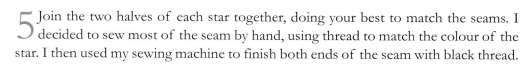

HINT

It is hard to see the foundation lines when you use black as the main fabric, so I suggest making one star block with a black background as a sample, and changing to a lighter coloured main fabric if black proves too difficult.

4 Each star is made in two pieces, which are then joined together. Following the instructions given in the Foundation Piecing chapter, pages 25–38, sew each half star. You will need to be careful when you add piece 3 – it is best to start with a large piece of fabric, around 1in (2.5cm) square, and trim it to size after it is sewn in place. I made eight stars at a time, so that I could spend a few minutes sewing and then press the work. If you make each star individually, you will spend a lot of time moving from sewing machine to ironing board and back again.

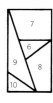

Star fabric-piecing sequence

5 Join the two halves of each star together, doing your best to match the seams. I decided to sew most of the seam by hand, using thread to match the colour of the star. I then used my sewing machine to finish both ends of the seam with black thread.

6 Now you can arrange the stars to give a pleasing effect. With so many bright colours, it can be hard to produce a balanced quilt. I decided to use the different colours in sequence – yellow, orange, green, pink, lilac, blue, turquoise, red – starting from the top left of the quilt. When you are happy with the arrangement, try stepping back a little and squinting – you may notice areas of the quilt which seem too bright or too dark. If so, swap a couple of blocks, although at this stage you would be swapping, for instance, a bright orange for a duller orange.

7 Next, sew the blocks together. You will need to take a lot of care at this stage to ensure that the blocks all end up square. To join two blocks together, lay them on top of each other and pass a pin through both blocks at one corner. Move the blocks carefully until the pin passes through a corner of each block. Do the same for the other corner, then open the blocks out to check that the stars are directly under each other. When you are happy that the blocks are in the right place, pin and stitch them together.

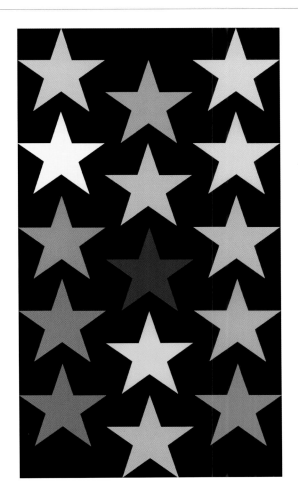

Different layouts of the stars

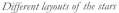

8 Continue sewing the blocks until you end up with five strips of six stars, which form the quilt top and sides, and a short strip of only three stars for the bottom. I decided to turn the stars at the side around so that they point upwards when they are on the bed. Press all the seams open.

9 Before you join the strips together to make the quilt top, you need to decide whether to offset the stars as I have done. If you look at the colour diagrams above you will see that staggering the centre row of stars adds movement to the quilt. To do this, you need to sew a small piece of black fabric to the top of the central row and similar pieces to the bottom of the outside rows.

10 Join together the strips which form the top of the quilt, then attach the sides and bottom of the quilt. Cut strips of black fabric approximately 2in (5cm) wide and attach these to the quilt top, then sew the sides and bottom onto these. Try to make sure that the stars are in line with each other across the quilt.

11 Lay the quilt on top of the wadding and backing fabric, then follow the instructions on pages 48–57 for quilting and binding. I used pellon as the wadding and plain black fabric for the backing. I quilted close to the patchwork stars using the walking foot on my sewing machine. The black border strips seemed to need some quilting, so I quilted small star shapes, using gold star stickers as my templates.

12 To bind the outside of the quilt, I cut strips of black fabric 1¼in (3cm) wide. I sewed florists' wire into the top binding and bottom corners, so that the quilt fits well on the bed.

HINT

Before you make these tiny star blocks, it is a good idea to try out the design in a large size. This will help you become familiar with the pattern, and enable you to try different colour combinations. The sample blocks make lovely greetings cards.

Large star template (actual size)

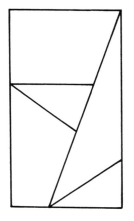
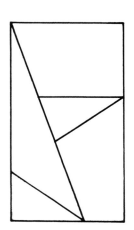

Greetings cards using the Stars design

quilt 19 KALEIDOSCOPE

When I bought this beautiful brass bed, I imagined it with a cream and gold quilt. This very sophisticated colour scheme uses only four different fabrics, and is ideal for a lady's bedroom. Although it was difficult to make, because the kaleidoscope design is quite complex, I am delighted with the final result.

Because of the complexity of the pattern it has many small seams, so I decided to use silk for the background fabric, to make a softer quilt. I was lucky enough to find a cream silk blouse in a charity shop and I used this for the background fabric, binding and backing. This still only used around half of the blouse, so I had plenty of silk left over for other quilts.

1 Measure your dolls' house bed and decide how many kaleidoscope blocks to make. I used 1in (2.5cm) blocks and needed 56 blocks altogether (see page 14 for guidelines). This quilt would also look effective with slightly larger blocks, say 1¼in (3cm) square, which would require fewer blocks to complete the quilt.

MATERIALS
- Fat eighth or 4in (10cm) length of three gold fabrics
- Cream silk, 10 × 40in (25 × 100cm)
- Fine, sew-in interfacing, 16 × 12in (40 × 30cm)
- Lightweight wadding, 10in (25cm) square
- Matching thread
- 56 tiny gold beads

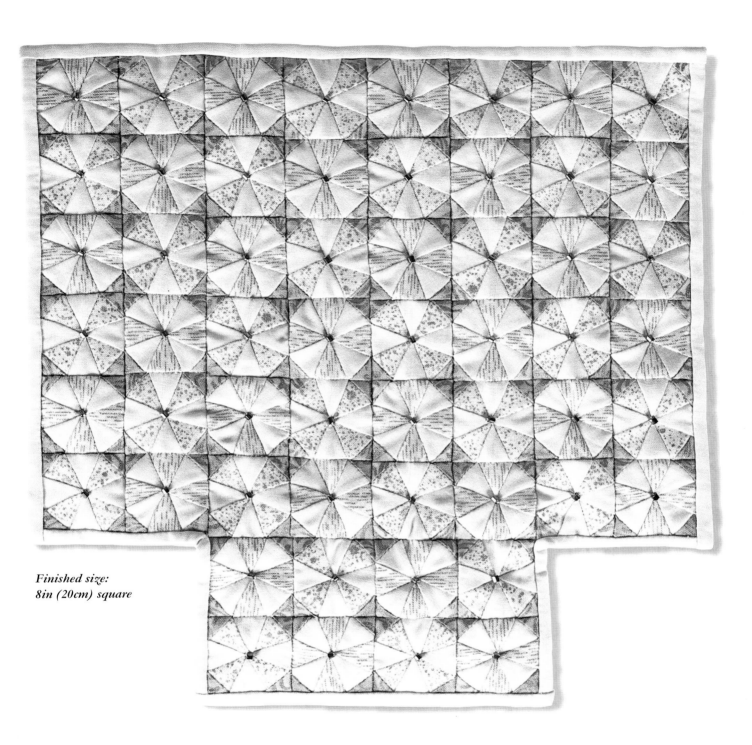

Finished size:
8in (20cm) square

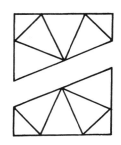

Kaleidoscope template (actual size)

2 As this is a complex design, I really recommend using a computer to produce the foundation patterns if you can – see the Using a Computer chapter, page 59, for guidance. Alternatively, draw the patterns on the interfacing, making sure that your lines are accurate. Each completed 1in (2.5cm) block requires two identical foundations which will be sewn together to make the square, so I needed 112 half-blocks.

> **HINT**
> Sharp needles are always important when you are making miniature quilts, but become essential when working with silk. Make sure your hand and machine needles are new, and as fine as you can work with – size 12 betweens for hand quilting and size 70/10 or even 60/8 for sewing machines.

3 The cream silk is used for nearly half of each patchwork block (pieces 2, 5, 8 and 11 in A blocks and pieces 1, 4, 7 and 10 in B blocks). I chose two pale cream and gold fabrics, one for A blocks and one for B blocks, and one darker gold fabric for the corner triangles of every block.

As I used just four different fabrics for the quilting, including the cream silk for the background fabric, I recommend buying a fat eighth of each one, or 4in (10cm) if you are buying off the roll. You could, of course, use many more different fabrics, in which case you would need less of each one.

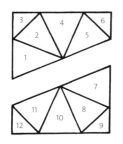

Kaleidoscope fabric-piecing sequence (actual size)

4 Following the instructions given in the Foundation Piecing chapter (page 25), make up two sample blocks in each of the A and B layouts – note that the placing of the cream background fabric changes. If you are happy with the fabrics you have chosen, carry on to make all 56 blocks, ensuring that you have 28 A blocks and 28 B blocks.

5 I found it helpful to make eight blocks at a time, and to cut my fabric into triangles before I began. The fabric cutting does not need to be very accurate, just as long as the pieces are big enough to cover the shape, leaving a reasonable seam allowance.

6 Joining together the two halves of each block is difficult, since there are many seams coming together at the middle. To join them, place two halves together, and pass a pin through at the ends of the central seam. Leave these pins vertical while you pin carefully along the seam, or tack the seam. Sew slowly, removing the pins as you go. You may need to unpick part of this seam and re-sew to get a good match. If you enjoy hand sewing, this seam could be sewn with tiny hand stitches instead of using a sewing machine. Press the central seam open, then trim all of the blocks.

7 Join the blocks together into long rows running down the bed, alternating A and B blocks. Note that the four central rows need eight blocks each, while the side rows need six blocks. As you join the blocks, try to match the seams of the dark gold fabric at the corners. Press the seams up on one row and down on the next.

8 Join the rows together to make the completed quilt top, taking great care with the pinning and sewing. Having the final seams running down the bed helps the quilt to drape over the sides of the bed.

9 Follow the instructions in the Finishing Your Quilt chapter, pages 48 and 54, for quilting and binding. For this quilt, I used more of the cream silk blouse for both the backing and the binding. Instead of hand or machine quilting, I decided to sew a small bead at the centre of each block. I used antique beads in dark gold, which matched the gold fabric in the corners of each block.

DESIGN VARIATION

If you choose fabrics with more colour contrast than cream and gold, you will see lovely curves appearing in the quilt design.

'A' block   'B' block

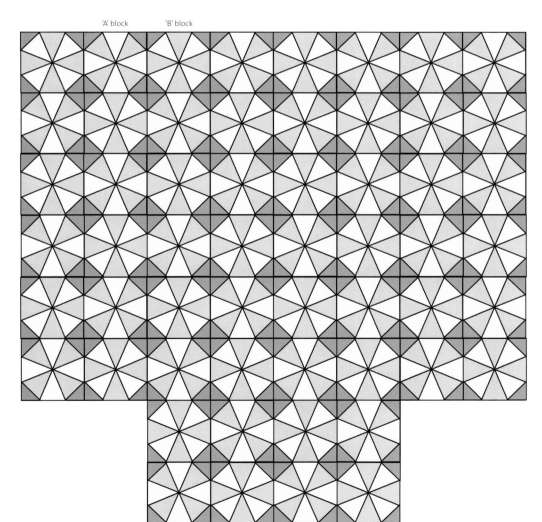

Kaleidoscope A and B blocks

quilt 20 AUTUMN LEAVES

The inspiration for this quilt came from the autumn leaves fabric which I have used for the backing and borders. I loved the colours, and the way the leaves all overlapped. Because the leaf design is rather complex, I chose to make just 28 blocks and to alternate these with plain cream squares. This not only made the quilt a little faster to make, it also produced a calmer effect than coloured leaves in every block.

This is the most complex quilt in the book, so I suggest that you try making an easier quilt first.

1 First measure your dolls' house bed and adjust the pattern to fit (see page 14 for guidelines). This quilt fits a single bed, and I used blocks ⅞in (2.2cm) square. You could make the leaf blocks a little larger if your bed is bigger, but for a smaller bed I recommend fewer blocks, since the leaf pattern is already quite small.

MATERIALS
- **Assortment of autumn-coloured fabrics, each 2in (5cm) square**
- **Cream fabric for background and alternate squares, 12 × 20in (30 × 50cm)**
- **Fine, sew-in interfacing, 16 × 12in (40 × 30cm)**
- **Lightweight wadding, 10in (25cm) square**
- **Patterned fabric for binding, 10 × 6in (25 × 15cm)**
- **Backing fabric, 10in (25cm) square**
- **Matching thread**
- **Brown embroidery cotton**
- **Florists' wire**

Finished size:
6¼ × 7¼in (16 × 19.5cm)

155

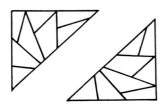

Autumn Leaves template
(actual size)

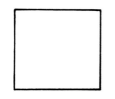

⅞in (2.2cm) square template

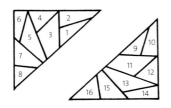

Autumn leaves fabric-piecing sequence

2 Prepare the foundation patterns, using fine, sew-in interfacing. Refer to the instructions for producing foundation fabric in the Using a Computer chapter (page 59), or draw the shapes on the interfacing using a ruler and sharp pencil. You will need 28 leaf blocks, which means 56 half leaves, and 28 'empty' squares for the cream blocks.

3 For this quilt, I sorted through my yellow, green and red fabrics, and chose colours that were similar to the border fabric. I deliberately chose a range of yellows – some more orange, some more mustard – as well as dull greens and rusty reds. You could of course use fewer fabrics, and use each one two or three times, but you will then need more of each fabric.

4 When it came to choosing a background fabric, I spent some time experimenting with different colours. Initially I planned to use dark brown, to give the effect of leaves fallen onto dark earth. However, I found that the leaves disappeared into the background, so decided that cream would be better.

HINT
Why not try a summer leaves quilt, with each leaf made from a different green fabric?

5 To make sure that the alternating cream squares were exactly the same size as the leaf blocks, I printed out 28 blocks from the computer onto interfacing, each ⅞in (2.2cm) square. I sewed these to the reverse side of the cream background fabric, then cut out the squares.

6 Making the leaf blocks will require patience and a few hours of sewing. Refer to the Foundation Piecing chapter (page 25) for detailed instructions on this method. Make sure that you use fabric pieces significantly larger than the finished section, as the shapes are awkward. I sewed all of the red leaves first, so that I could use red thread. I then sewed the yellow leaves, followed by the green.

7 The most difficult part of the quilt is joining the two halves of each leaf together. You will need to pin very carefully, making sure that all three corners of each half-leaf meet up. Sew slowly along the central seam, being prepared to unpick a little of the seam if it has not matched up well enough. I used coloured thread to match the leaves for most of the central seam, then sewed the final part of the seam with cream thread. Press this central seam open.

8 When all the leaves are complete, spend some time arranging them. See the diagram for the placement of the red, yellow and green leaves and look carefully at the colours you have used, to make sure that brighter fabrics are spread evenly throughout the quilt. You will see that I chose to rotate some of the leaf blocks, to give the impression of autumn leaves swirling in the air.

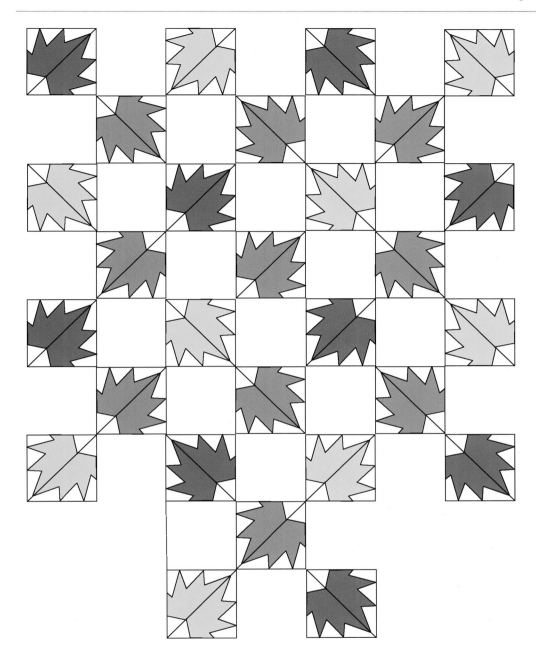

9 Join the blocks together into seven long strips, running down the bed. The leaf blocks alternate with plain blocks. Note that the three central strips will each have nine blocks rather than seven. Press the seam allowances towards the plain cream squares, then join the strips to make the complete quilt top.

10 Follow the instructions in Finishing Your Quilt (page 39) for completing the quilt. I spent some time experimenting with different quilting designs, and finally decided just to quilt a leaf shape in the cream squares. There is no quilting in the patchwork squares, as quilting seemed to detract from the sharp leaf shape.

Quilting template for Autumn Leaves (actual size)

To quilt the leaf shape, I printed out leaves a little bit smaller than the plain squares – you can trace the smaller leaf shape shown left. I then used a tiny piece of double-sided sticky tape to fix the leaf pattern temporarily onto the quilt top, and slowly machine sewed around it. I started at the bottom of the leaf, and finished by adding a stalk and some veins. In the diagram on page 157 you will see that the quilted leaf shapes face in different directions, just as the patchwork leaves do. The quilting on this little quilt took over four hours but it was worth it, as I am very happy with the result.

11 Next, sew the binding around the outside of the quilt. I cut 1¼in (3.2cm) strips of the autumn leaves fabric, and used the binding method described on page 54. You could use the cream background fabric for the border, or choose one of the leaf colours to set off the patchwork. I used florists' wire in the top binding and the short L-shaped sections at the foot of the bed, which helps the quilt to keep its shape on the bed (see instructions for this on page 57).

HINT
Since this is a complex design, it would be helpful to make a larger leaf before you try the small ones. Use the large leaf diagram below and practise adding the fabric pieces in the right order. Join the two halves of your sample together, matching the seams carefully.

Large leaf block (actual size)

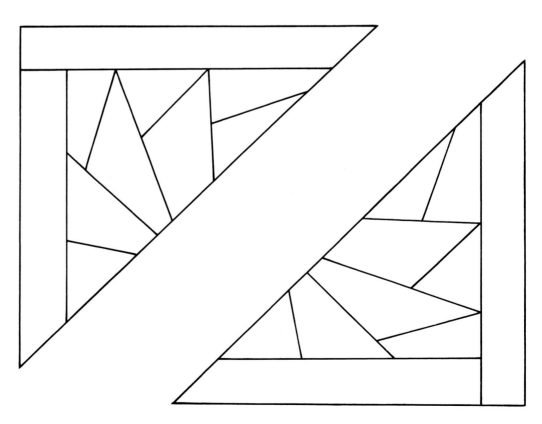

12 As a finishing touch, you could embroider stems on the patchwork leaves using brown embroidery cotton, as I have done.

I turned sample blocks into a small wallhanging, shown below, by adding strips of the autumn leaves fabric.

GALLERY OF QUILTS

When I started to write this book, I wanted to include photographs of quilts made by other people as well as my own quilts. The main reason was to show the variety of excellent work that is being done by miniaturists all around the world. I was overwhelmed by the response to my letters in magazines and e-mails on quilting websites. The standard of work is so high, and the number of quilts I looked at so great, that it was very difficult to choose just a few to include in this chapter.

The quilts come from Australia, the Netherlands, the United Kingdom and the USA. Sometimes the quilter has only made one dolls' house quilt, sometimes she has made many. I have included a selection of different styles and techniques, as well as a range of colours, but left the miniaturists to describe their quilts in their own words.

Claire Brach
Australia
Satin Tulips
8 × 8½in (20 × 21 cm)
Machine embroidery
Made to match the furnishings of a classic dolls' house

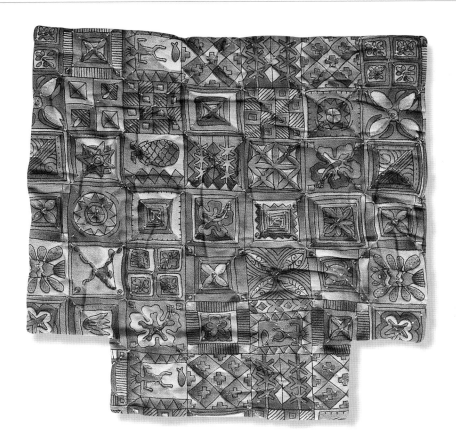

Claire Brach
Australia
Safari
8 ×8½in (20 ×21cm)
Machine quilting
This little quilt was inspired
by the printed fabric

Claire Brach
Australia
Victorian taffeta
7¾ ×8in (19.5 ×20cm)
Machine quilted
In winter, Victorian beds
had both a bedspread and a
coverlet for warmth. I used
three layers of pellon so
that the machine quilting
really stands out

Lesley Conning
England
6⅝in (16.5 cm) square
Foundation pieced over paper by
machine. Layered with
lightweight interlining and
machine quilted
Made just for fun after
seeing some 1/12 scale
quilts at an exhibition.
I borrowed a rubber stamp
of a log cabin block and
used it to produce the
foundation patterns

Patricia Cox
USA
Baltimore-style Bride's Quilt
6½ × 6¼in (16.5 × 16cm).
Hand appliqué, broderie perse
and hand quilting
Full-size Baltimore quilts are
my area of research but
when this particular fabric
was printed I decided to
make a miniature for my
dolls' house

Patricia Cox
USA
*Bridal Whole
Cloth Quilt*
6½ × 8½in
(16.5 × 21.5cm)
*Hand quilting
with handmade
tatted lace*
This quilt was
made as a replica of
a full-size whole
cloth quilt

Jenny Grant
Australia
7 × 9in
(18 × 23cm)
Silk, hand-pieced
'English patchwork'
using paper templates
Made for a 1/12
scale Edwardian
dolls' house

Patricia Cox
USA
Log Cabin Pineapple quilt
5¾in (14.5cm) square.
Machine pieced over a
paper foundation
The quilt was made
during a period when
I was experimenting
with different styles
of quilting in miniature

Jenny Grant
Australia
7⅝ × 9⅜in (19.5 × 24cm)
Hand pieced 'English
patchwork' using paper
templates. Fabrics are mostly
Liberty prints
Made for a 1/12 scale
Edwardian-style dolls' house

Sheila Grantham
England
*Red, White and Blue Log
Cabin Design for the Late
Nineteenth Century*
6in (15cm) square.
*Hand-sewn using hand-dyed silk
habotai. Foundation method on
tear-away paper*
Based on a full-size quilt
thought to have been made
by Lillie A. Miller Rohrbach,
a Mennonite woman born in
1876 in Pennyslvania. The
original quilt is featured in
Log Cabin Quilts published
by Rodale Press Inc. 1997.
This quilt won first prize in
the patchwork quilt section
of the Miniature
Needlework Society
competition in 2001

Sheila Grantham
England
*Peacock Feather Hexagonal
Quilt*
6in (15cm) square
*Hand-sewn over paper
templates using hand-dyed silk
habotai. Knotting was used to
quilt the layers*
The colours in the quilt
were inspired by a peacock's
feather. This quilt won first
prize in the novice section
for patchwork quilts in the
Miniature Needlework
Society competition in 1999

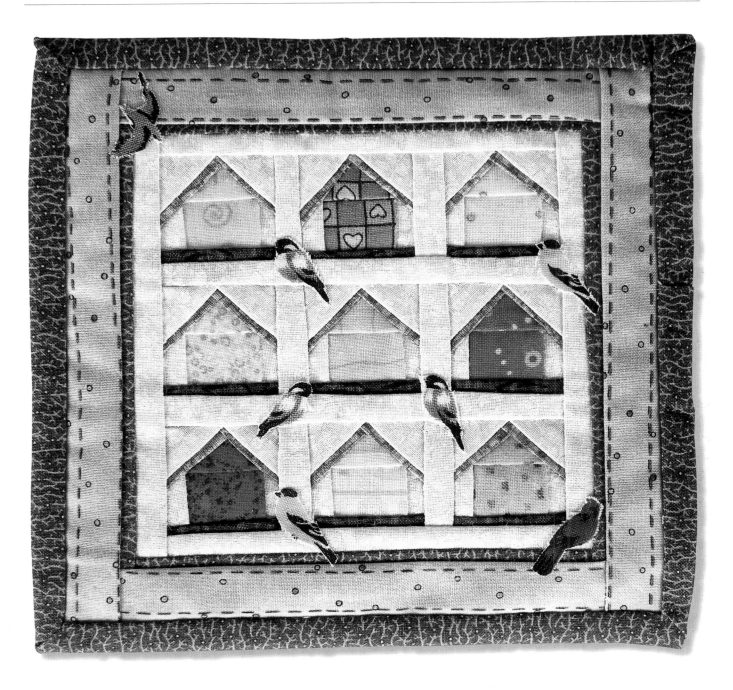

Els Greven
The Netherlands
Welcome Home
5¹/₂in (14cm) square
Paper piecing
I was inspired by the many
quilt shows I visited, and
plan to make a gallery full
of dolls' house quilts

167

Patty Groenewegen
The Netherlands
Ode aan Geert
5½in (14 cm) square
Paper piecing by hand
I made this little quilt for a
competition in 2001, and
used scraps of fabric given
to me by my friend Geert. I
was very pleased to win first
prize in the competition

Diana Harbour
England
Snail's Trail
6⅝in (17cm) square
Foundation pieced by hand
I like scrappy quilts so I
used 128 different
red/mauve/blue fabrics for
the patches. I traced the
foundations onto an old
cotton handkerchief

Diana Harbour
England
Log Cabin
6⅜in (16cm) square
Foundation pieced by hand
and hand quilted
This is the first miniature
quilt I made using fabric left
over from a full-size,
double-bed quilt

169

Diana Harbour
England
Flying Geese
4¾in square (12cm) square
Foundation pieced by hand
I designed this quilt to see
how small a patch size I
could sew using traditional
patchwork cotton fabrics

Wendy Lievesley
Australia
Mini Tumblers No 3 (1993)
7¼ × 8¼in (18.5 × 21cm).
Hand pieced and
hand quilted
One of a series of quilts
made to show various
arrangements of colour
using a single pattern shape

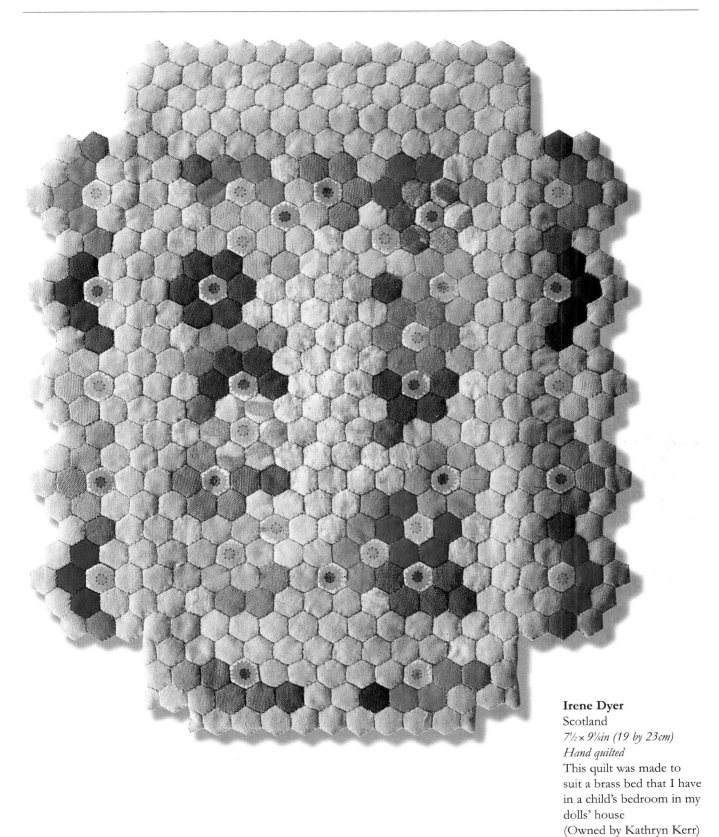

Irene Dyer
Scotland
7½ × 9⅛in (19 by 23cm)
Hand quilted
This quilt was made to
suit a brass bed that I have
in a child's bedroom in my
dolls' house
(Owned by Kathryn Kerr)

Wendy Lievesley
Australia
*Miniature Flying
Geese (1992)*
*7⅛ × 9½in
(19.5 × 24.5cm)*
*Foundation pieced by
machine on paper, hand
quilted*
Pattern from *Miniature
Quilts* magazine. I
enjoyed the
foundation piecing
technique and have
used it for many other
quilts since 1992

Wendy Lievesley
Australia
Samples of Purple (2001)
7¼ × 9in (18.5 × 23cm)
Hand pieced and hand quilted
This design resulted from
playing with shapes drawn
on graph paper and purple
fabric samples

Jo Rednall
England
Friends Forever
4⅛ × 5⅛in (10.5 × 13cm)
Pieced by bonding to fabric top.
Four-layer sandwich of organza,
pieced top, wadding and backing.
Free machine quilted with
metallic thread
Made in shades of pale pink
and green to match the
colour scheme of my friend
Sheila Sinclair's house. She is
furnishing her 1/12 scale
dolls' house with miniature
versions of the contents of
her home

Janine Ridler
England
Boston
6 × 8in (15 × 20cm)
Machine pieced, hand quilted
One of several quilts I made using the same four materials in different ways. I chose dark colours as a change from the more feminine colours often used in quilts

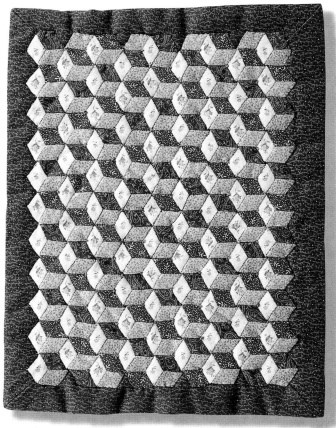

Diane Whitehead
England
Mini Tumbling Blocks
6½ × 8½in (6.5 × 22 cm)
English paper piecing using ¼in (6mm) diamonds
The quilt was designed to fit a 1/12 scale double bed made by my husband for my dolls' house. It was started at a workshop with Anthea Linacre in London and took over five years to make. The wadding (batting) is a piece of fine flannel material and the quilt is 'tied' with French knots

Annie Whitsed
Australia
Miniature Amish Quilt (1986)
5 × 5in (12 × 12cm)
Machine pieced, hand quilted
I made this miniature Amish quilt as a follow up to an Amish colour workshop

175

Annie Whitsed
Australia
Nature's Jewels (1994)
5⅞ × 7⅞ in
(15 × 19.5 cm)
Machine-pieced crazy
patchwork with hand
embroidery and
embellishments
Prize-winning quilt
made as an entry
for the miniature
quilt section of the
Mt Gravat show

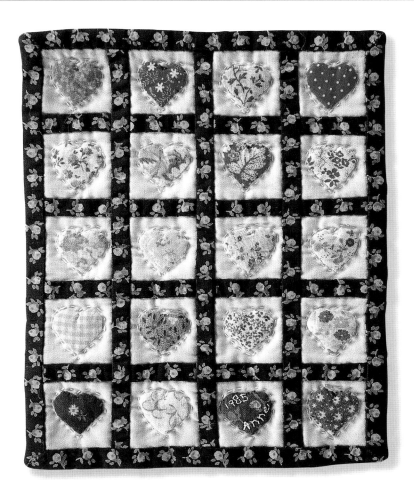

Annie Whitsed
Australia
Hearts (1985)
5⅛ × 6⅜in (13 × 16cm)
Hand appliqué, hand quilted
Made from sample swatches to experiment with hand appliqué as a technique for making miniatures

Sarah Williams
Australia
Garden Trellis Wallhanging (2001)
3 × 2¼in (7.5 × 7cm)
Machine pieced,
hand quilted
I had some fabrics with tiny leaves and flowers, and wondered if I could make a wallhanging in 1/12 scale

bibliography

General Quilting Books

Anderson, Alex
Fabric Shopping with Alex Anderson
C&T Publishing Inc., 2000
ISBN 1 57120 089 4
A great introduction to types of fabric and the use of colour in quilts. While the quantities of fabric to buy don't apply to dolls' house quilts, the rest of the book is very relevant.

Fassett, Kaffe and Lucy, Liza Prior
Patchwork
Ebury Press, 1997
ISBN 0 0918 5171 8
The patchwork designs are quite simple – what sets them apart from most quilts is Kaffe Fassett's use of colour, which is truly inspiring.

Leone, Diane
The New Sampler Quilt
C&T Publishing Inc., 1993
ISBN 1 57120 011 8
Lots of clear photographs and illustrations make this a good starting point for beginners. Some of the simpler blocks would work well in dolls' house quilts.

Pahl, Ellen (Editor)
The Quilter's Ultimate Visual Guide
Rodale Press, Inc., 1997
ISBN 0 87596 987 9
A comprehensive explanation of many facets of patchwork and quilting, illustrated by detailed drawings and photographs.

Rodale Quilt Book Editors
Flawless Hand Quilting
Rodale Press Inc., 1999
ISBN 0 87596 760 4
If, like me, hand quilting is not your strong point, I recommend reading this book. With its clear photographs at every step, everyone can attempt hand quilting.

Wickell, Janet
Teach Yourself Quilting
Hodder & Stoughton, 2000
ISBN 0 658 00494 8
A great introduction to patchwork, quilting and appliqué, with clear explanations of foundation piecing.

Colour

Most libraries have books on colour theory. However, many of them are written for artists rather than quilters. Three books which I found particularly useful are:

McKelvey, Susan
Creative Ideas for Color and Fabric
Rodale Press Inc., 1996
ISBN 0 87596 726 4
Starting with an explanation of colour theory, this book encourages readers to analyse their fabric collections. It contains many useful hints on selecting colours to achieve the effect you want.

Perry, Gai
Color from the Heart
C&T Publishing Inc., 1999
ISBN 1 57120 071 1
This workbook takes the reader through seven lessons in using colour in quilts. Since each quilt is shown in various colourways, the effect of choosing different fabrics for a quilt becomes clear.

Seely, Ann and Stewart, Joyce
Colour Magic for Quilters
Rodale Press Inc., 1997
ISBN 0 87596 95 2
This book gives an excellent explanation of colour theory, and contains many examples of different colour combinations. The authors show many quilt designs using fabrics, and include a number of quilt projects with detailed instructions.

Dolls' House Books

Dodge, Venus A.
Dolls' House Needlecrafts
David & Charles, 1995
ISBN 0 7153 0169 1
My adult fascination with dolls' houses began with this book, so it remains a personal favourite. There are many ideas for items to make for your dolls' house, including simple patchwork quilts.

Travis, Dinah
The Miniature Quilt
B.T. Batsford Ltd, 1998
ISBN 0 7134 8123 9
The 20 quilts in this book are all made using different techniques, including patchwork. Instructions are also given for dolls' house beds.

Warner, Pamela
Miniature Embroidery for the Victorian Dolls' House
GMC Publications, 1998
ISBN 1 86108 095 6
Lots of great ideas for your dolls' house, including rugs, cushions and curtains.

Mauer, Walt
Amish People, Amish Portrait
Garden Spot Gifts Inc., 1998
ISBN 1 890541 36 2
This short book explains the history of the Amish people and outlines their way of life.

Useful websites for buying beds or quilts

www.dollshouseemporium.com
www.miniaturesbyclaire.com
www.dijon.co.uk
www.craft-club.com
www.hobby.uk.com

glossary

Baking parchment
Non-stick paper, usually a heavier weight than greaseproof paper.

Batting
Also called wadding, this is the central layer in a quilt which adds warmth to the patchwork top. Wadding can be made from wool, cotton, polyester or silk.

'Betweens' needle
A short, fine needle with a small eye, traditionally used for quilting.

Chain-piecing
This is a quick method of sewing patchwork blocks where you sew each seam without cutting the sewing machine threads between each block.

Charm squares
Small pieces of fabric sold as a pack, often following a theme. This is a good way of buying a variety of prints to use in miniature quilts.

Conversational prints
Fabrics with pictures rather than geometric or floral designs. Most conversational prints are too large for use in dolls' house quilts, but occasionally you may find one that is suitable.

Cutting board
Special cutting mat, sometimes called a 'self-healing mat' which is used with a rotary cutter. The cutting board is not damaged by the rotary cutter, and does not make the rotary cutter blunt.

Fat eighths and fat quarters
Fabric shops often sell 'fat quarters' and 'fat eighths' of patchwork fabric, as well as fabric on the roll.

Fat eighth
A fat eighth is half a yard or half a metre of fabric, cut in quarters to give approximately 10 × 20in (25 × 50cm).

Fat quarter
A fat quarter is half a yard or half a metre of fabric, cut in half to give approximately 20in (50cm) square.

Florists' wire
Very fine wire coated in green paper. Sold for wiring flowers for arrangements, it can be sewn into the binding of miniature quilts to help them sit well on a bed.

Freezer paper
This heavily waxed paper can be ironed onto the reverse of fabric to stabilize it while printing designs from a computer. It is also useful for making quilting templates, as it can be ironed onto the quilt, then peeled off carefully after use.

'Loft'
Wadding (batting) fibres are compressed when they are quilted. The 'loft' describes how well wadding springs back after quilting.

Mitred corners
Borders sewn with a 45° seam at the corners are said to have 'mitred corners'. These are hard to sew, but look effective.

Pellon
Lightweight polyester wadding (*see also* batting).

Quilter's rule
A large, flat ruler marked with either inch or centimetre squares, used with a rotary cutter and cutting board to cut strips of fabric.

Rotary cutter
This special tool makes cutting strips of fabric for binding quilts an easy task. The cutting blade turns as the cutter is pushed along the fabric, giving a clean cut through up to six layers of fabric at a time.

Sashing
Strips of fabric sewn between patchwork blocks to separate them. Sashing strips can draw attention to patchwork designs and make the quilt appear more restful.

Scale of print
Fabric prints are either large-scale, medium-scale or small-scale. This refers to the size of the pattern printed on the fabric.

Stab stitching
Method of hand quilting where the needle is 'stabbed' through all the layers to the back of the work, then returned to the front. Useful when quilting over seam allowances.

Stash
Quilters' term for a fabric collection. Many quilters abide by the motto 'She (or he) who collects the most fabric, wins!'

Tone-on-tone prints
Fabrics where the design is printed in the same colour as the background, only a little paler or darker. Tone-on-tone prints often have small motifs which make them especially suitable for dolls' house patchwork.

Walking foot
Also called an 'even-feed foot', this sewing machine attachment feeds fabric from the top as well as underneath. The result is even quilting with no puckers, since all the layers pass under the needle at the same rate.

about the author

Sarah Williams grew up in Scotland and spent many hours as a child sewing and playing with her dolls' house. She learnt knitting, dressmaking and embroidery from her mother, who had trained as a domestic science teacher and encouraged Sarah to develop her skills.

In her teens, Sarah considered studying embroidery at university, but decided instead to study business. This led to a career in information management in the UK public sector. During this time, Sarah made patchwork cot quilts for friends' babies, and visited quilt shows with her mother.

In 1997 Sarah renovated a dolls' house for her daughter, and re-discovered the fascinating world of miniatures. Instructions for two small projects suitable for a child to play with were published in *Dolls' House World* magazine during 1997.

At the end of 1998 Sarah moved to Australia with her family and took a break from work to spend time with her young children. This gave her more time to spend on miniatures, and she began experimenting with miniature patchwork.

Sarah lives in Sydney, Australia with her husband, two children and lots of tropical fish.

index

BOOKS

ART TECHNIQUES
Oil Paintings from your Garden: A Guide for Beginners — *Rachel Shirley*

CRAFTS
American Patchwork Designs in Needlepoint — *Melanie Tacon*
Bargello: A Fresh Approach to Florentine Embroidery — *Brenda Day*
Beginning Picture Marquetry — *Lawrence Threadgold*
Blackwork: A New Approach — *Brenda Day*
Celtic Cross Stitch Designs — *Carol Phillipson*
Celtic Knotwork Designs — *Sheila Sturrock*
Celtic Knotwork Handbook — *Sheila Sturrock*
Celtic Spirals and Other Designs — *Sheila Sturrock*
Complete Pyrography — *Stephen Poole*
Creating Made-to-Measure Knitwear: A Revolutionary Approach to
  Knitwear Design — *Sylvia Wynn*
Creative Backstitch — *Helen Hall*
Creative Embroidery Techniques Using Colour Through Gold
  — *Daphne J. Ashby & Jackie Woolsey*
The Creative Quilter: Techniques and Projects — *Pauline Brown*
Cross-Stitch Designs from China — *Carol Phillipson*
Decoration on Fabric: A Sourcebook of Ideas — *Pauline Brown*
Decorative Beaded Purses — *Enid Taylor*
Designing and Making Cards — *Glennis Gilruth*
Glass Engraving Pattern Book — *John Everett*
Glass Painting — *Emma Sedman*
Handcrafted Rugs — *Sandra Hardy*
How to Arrange Flowers: A Japanese Approach to English Design
  — *Taeko Marvelly*
How to Make First-Class Cards — *Debbie Brown*
An Introduction to Crewel Embroidery — *Mave Glenny*
Making and Using Working Drawings for Realistic Model Animals
  — *Basil F. Fordham*
Making Character Bears — *Valerie Tyler*
Making Decorative Screens — *Amanda Howes*
Making Fabergé-Style Eggs — *Denise Hopper*
Making Fairies and Fantastical Creatures — *Julie Sharp*
Making Greetings Cards for Beginners — *Pat Sutherland*
Making Hand-Sewn Boxes: Techniques and Projects — *Jackie Woolsey*
Making Mini Cards, Gift Tags & Invitations — *Glennis Gilruth*
Making Soft-Bodied Dough Characters — *Patricia Hughes*
Natural Ideas for Christmas: Fantastic Decorations to Make
  — *Josie Cameron-Ashcroft & Carol Cox*
New Ideas for Crochet: Stylish Projects for the Home — *Darsha Capaldi*
Papercraft Projects for Special Occasions — *Sine Chesterman*
Patchwork for Beginners — *Pauline Brown*
Pyrography Designs — *Norma Gregory*
Pyrography Handbook (Practical Crafts) — *Stephen Poole*
Rose Windows for Quilters — *Angela Besley*
Rubber Stamping with Other Crafts — *Lynne Garner*
Silk Painting — *Jill Clay*
Sponge Painting — *Ann Rooney*
Stained Glass: Techniques and Projects — *Mary Shanahan*

Step-by-Step Pyrography Projects for the Solid Point Machine — *Norma Gregory*
Tassel Making for Beginners — *Enid Taylor*
Tatting Collage — *Lindsay Rogers*
Tatting Patterns — *Lyn Morton*
Temari: A Traditional Japanese Embroidery Technique — *Margaret Ludlow*
Trip Around the World: 25 Patchwork, Quilting and Appliqué Projects
  — *Gail Lawther*
Trompe l'Oeil: Techniques and Projects — *Jan Lee Johnson*
Tudor Treasures to Embroider — *Pamela Warner*
Wax Art — *Hazel Marsh*

DOLLS' HOUSES AND MINIATURES
1/12 Scale Character Figures for the Dolls' House — *James Carrington*
Americana in 1/12 Scale: 50 Authentic Projects
  — *Joanne Ogreenc & Mary Lou Santovec*
Architecture for Dolls' Houses — *Joyce Percival*
The Authentic Georgian Dolls' House — *Brian Long*
A Beginners' Guide to the Dolls' House Hobby — *Jean Nisbett*
Celtic, Medieval and Tudor Wall Hangings in 1/12 Scale Needlepoint
  — *Sandra Whitehead*
Creating Decorative Fabrics: Projects in 1/12 Scale — *Janet Storey*
The Dolls' House 1/24 Scale: A Complete Introduction — *Jean Nisbett*
Dolls' House Accessories, Fixtures and Fittings — *Andrea Barham*
Dolls' House Furniture: Easy-to-Make Projects in 1/12 Scale — *Freida Gray*
Dolls' House Makeovers — *Jean Nisbett*
Dolls' House Window Treatments — *Eve Harwood*
Easy to Make Dolls' House Accessories — *Andrea Barham*
Edwardian-Style Hand-Knitted Fashion for 1/12 Scale Dolls — *Yvonne Wakefield*
How to Make Your Dolls' House Special: Fresh Ideas for Decorating
  — *Beryl Armstrong*
Make Your Own Dolls' House Furniture — *Maurice Harper*
Making Dolls' House Furniture — *Patricia King*
Making Georgian Dolls' Houses — *Derek Rowbottom*
Making Miniature Chinese Rugs and Carpets — *Carol Phillipson*
Making Miniature Food and Market Stalls — *Angie Scarr*
Making Miniature Gardens — *Freida Gray*
Making Miniature Oriental Rugs & Carpets — *Meik & Ian McNaughton*
Making Period Dolls' House Accessories — *Andrea Barham*
Making Tudor Dolls' Houses — *Derek Rowbottom*
Making Victorian Dolls' House Furniture — *Patricia King*
Medieval and Tudor Needlecraft: Knights and Ladies in 1/12 Scale
  — *Sandra Whitehead*
Miniature Bobbin Lace — *Roz Snowden*
Miniature Embroidery for the Georgian Dolls' House — *Pamela Warner*
Miniature Embroidery for the Tudor and Stuart Dolls' House — *Pamela Warner*
Miniature Embroidery for the Victorian Dolls' House — *Pamela Warner*
Miniature Needlepoint Carpets — *Janet Granger*
More Miniature Oriental Rugs & Carpets — *Meik & Ian McNaughton*
Needlepoint 1/12 Scale: Design Collections for the Dolls' House — *Felicity Price*
New Ideas for Miniature Bobbin Lace — *Roz Snowden*
Patchwork Quilts for the Dolls' House: 20 Projects in 1/12 Scale
  — *Sarah Williams*

GARDENING

PHOTOGRAPHY

TOYMAKING

UPHOLSTERY

MAGAZINES

WOODTURNING ◆ WOODCARVING ◆ FURNITURE & CABINETMAKING
THE ROUTER ◆ NEW WOODWORKING ◆ THE DOLLS' HOUSE MAGAZINE
OUTDOOR PHOTOGRAPHY ◆ BLACK & WHITE PHOTOGRAPHY
TRAVEL PHOTOGRAPHY
MACHINE KNITTING NEWS ◆ BUSINESSMATTERS

The above represents a selection of the titles currently published or scheduled to be published.
All are available direct from the Publishers or through bookshops, newsagents and specialist retailers.
To place an order, or to obtain a complete catalogue, contact:

GMC Publications,
Castle Place, 166 High Street, Lewes, East Sussex BN7 1XU, United Kingdom
Tel: 01273 488005 Fax: 01273 478606
E-mail: pubs@thegmcgroup.com

Orders by credit card are accepted